EYEWITNESS

INDONESIAN
PHRASE BOOK

DORLING KINDERSLEY
LONDON · NEW YORK · SYDNEY · MOSCOW

A DORLING KINDERSLEY BOOK

Compiled by Lexus Ltd with
Oking Gandamihardhja and Nigel Phillips
Printed in Great Britain by Cambus Litho

First published in Great Britain in 1998
by Dorling Kindersley Limited
9 Henrietta Street, London WC2E 8PS

Copyright 1998 © Dorling Kindersley Limited, London

A CIP catalogue record is available from the British Library.
ISBN 0 7513 1097 2

Picture Credits
Jacket: all images special photography Clive Streeter and
Michael Spencer except BRITSTOCK IFA: Cassio back left;
M.Gottschalk front bottom right; Günter Graefenhain front
centre below; H.Schimidbauer front top left, spine; FFOTOGRAFF:
Charles Aithie front bottom left; Patricia Aithie front top right;
NEIL SETCHFIELD: front centre left, front centre right.

CONTENTS

PREFACE

This *Eyewitness Travel Guide Phrase Book* has been compiled
by experts to meet the general needs of tourists and business
travellers. Arranged under headings such as Hotels, Motoring
and so forth, the ample selection of useful words and phrases
is supported by a 2,000-line mini-dictionary. There is also an
extensive menu guide listing approximately 500 dishes or
methods of cooking and presentation.

Typical replies to questions you may ask during your journey,
and the signs or instructions you may see or hear, are shown
in tinted boxes. The pronunciation of words and phrases in the
main text is indicated in English sound syllables at the bottom
of each righthand page. The Introduction gives basic
guidelines to Indonesian pronunciation.

Eyewitness Travel Guides are recognised as the world's best
travel guides. Each title features specially commissioned colour
photographs, cutaways of major buildings, 3-D aerial views
and detailed maps, plus information on sights, events, hotels,
restaurants, shopping and entertainment.

INTRODUCTION

PRONUNCIATION

When speaking Indonesian, the same value should be given to all syllables as they are generally evenly stressed. Indonesian uses the Roman alphabet and letters are pronounced as in English with a few exceptions. Remember the points below and your pronunciation will be even closer to the correct Indonesian.

a	sounds like a cross between the 'a' in 'father' and the 'u' in 'mud'
ai	like the 'i' in 'high'
au	like the 'ow' in 'now'
c	'ch' as in 'church'
e	like the 'e' in 'herd'
<u>e</u>	'e' as in 'bed' – this is shown with an underline
g	'g' as in 'go'
h	pronounced more strongly than in English; the exception is at the end of a word when it is pronounced more softly
i	like the 'ee' in 'meet'
kh	like the 'ch' in 'Bach'
ng	'ng' as in 'long'
ny	like the 'ny' in 'canyon'
o	like the 'o' in 'hot'
sy	'sh' as in 'shoot'
u	like the 'oo' in 'fool'
v	'f' as in 'first'

At the bottom of each righthand page of the phrase sections, you will find a pronunciation guide for easy reference. Also in the phrase sections, words spelt and pronounced the same as English are indicated in quotes, for example 'tip'. Those that are spelt the same but pronounced differently have the pronunciation indicated in italics, for example **menu** (*menoo*).

'YOU' AND 'YOUR'

Indonesian does not have a general word like 'you', that can be used to address anyone. The word used for 'you' depends on the age and status of the person you are speaking to and the situation. If the person is older than you or the same age, it is best to use the polite words **Bapak** or **Pak** (father), and **Ibu** or **Bu** (mother). These can be used with or without the person's name. If the person is younger than you and has a job like a waiter or waitress, you should use **Adik** or **Dik** (younger brother/sister). There are other words corresponding to 'you', but **anda**, the formal equivalent of 'you' is most often used when meeting someone for the first time. The words corresponding to 'you' also mean 'your' in Indonesian.

'TO BE'

Indonesian has no equivalent of the verb 'to be'. So, for example, 'I am hungry' is translated as **saya lapar** (*I hungry*), and 'I am a teacher' as **saya guru** (*I teacher*).

CROSS-CULTURAL NOTES

RELIGION AND POLITICS

About 90% of Indonesians are Muslims, the rest being mainly Christians, with smaller numbers of Buddhists and Hindus. Indonesians are required by law to hold one of five officially recognised religions, and a much larger proportion than in Britain take their religion seriously. Therefore, if foreigners express anti-religious views they will almost certainly offend people. Furthermore, atheism is identified with communism, which is officially banned and popularly condemned.

It would also cause offence if a visitor were to criticise the President and the government openly, although it is quite acceptable for Indonesians to criticise the government in private conversation.

MEETING INDONESIANS

Indonesians enjoy socialising, often visiting the homes of friends and relations without prior arrangement (not many homes have telephones), and spending a good deal of time in friendly conversation. Staying in by oneself to read or going to the cinema alone is much less common than in Britain. Such behaviour can be thought a sign of unsociability or aloofness.

When visiting a house, people take their shoes off at the door. (This is also done when entering a mosque.) The host or hostess is almost certain to serve tea or something else to drink and a light snack. Guests should wait to drink and eat until the host invites them to. It is impolite to refuse food or drink placed before you, although in most cases a symbolic sip or spoonful will be sufficient to avoid offence.

Indonesians often greet each other with **apa kabar?** (literally, 'what's the news?') to which the reply is **kabar baik** ('the news is good'). Less formally, they may ask **mau ke mana?** which literally means 'where are you going?'. Indonesians often translate their greeting into English for a Westerner, and their intention should be taken to be a 'hello' rather than an intrusion into one's private affairs. A general reply such as **jalan-jalan** ('going for a walk') will suffice. You may sometimes be greeted by Muslims with **assalam alaikum**, especially if you are inside a house or room, and they are waiting to come in. Even though you may not be a Muslim, it is polite to reply with: **walaikum salam**. Indeed, some people may not feel at ease to enter until they have received this greeting.

ADDRESSING INDONESIANS

In general, people younger than yourself should be addressed as **adik** (**dik** for short). If you are not sure whether they might be a little older or not, it is best to assume that they are and call them **bang** (**mas** in Java), if they are male, and **kak** (**mbak** in Java) if they are female. If, however, the person you are addressing has a job similar in status to yours, use the respectful terms **Bapak/Pak** for men and **Ibu/Bu** for women, even if he/she is younger than you. People quite obviously much older than yourself should be addressed as **Pak**, if they are male, and **Ibu**, if female, regardless of status. There are many regional variations which you will come across, but the above examples are universally understood. If you know a person's name, use it with the appropriate term when addressing him/her, eg **Ibu Maria, Pak Oking**. Small children can be addressed as **nak** or by name. (See also page 6: 'YOU AND YOUR'.)

APPEARANCES

Most Indonesians like to wear clean, well-ironed clothes and have well-groomed hair. Even quite poor people make an effort to look smart and so tourists who wear frayed, dirty clothing are not admired. Shorts are not worn by adults, except for sport or manual work, and women's clothes are in general more discreet and unrevealing than what is commonly worn in the West. Both men and women should keep their shoulders covered and skirts should cover the knees.

PERSONAL CONDUCT

Indonesians treat their elders with respect, using deferential forms of speech and behaviour. Public disagreement with one's superiors is also avoided, although this attitude is stronger among some ethnic groups (eg the Javanese) than others. In general, Indonesian behaviour is characterised by restraint in order to maintain a general state of harmony. Open displays of emotion, therefore, whether hysterical laughter, anger or affection, are not generally approved of. Couples, even if married, do not hold hands or kiss in public. However, members of the same sex in Indonesia are far more relaxed with each other physically than their counterparts in the West. It is a perfectly usual sight to see two young women or two young men walking hand in hand or sitting at a coffee shop with one massaging the other's neck.

It is offensive to use the left hand for eating, for giving, receiving or pointing at things, for shaking hands with people or waving to them, or for hailing buses and taxis. In cases when using the left hand is either unavoidable or more practicable, saying **maaf** ('sorry') should prevent any offence being taken. Indonesians shake hands with a fairly light grasp, and some women do not shake hands at all, but just smile and nod.

It is rude to point your finger at someone you are talking to. The Javanese point to things or people using the right thumb, not the index finger. When beckoning, people use all the fingers, palm downwards. It is insulting to touch anyone on the head. When passing directly in front of someone, it is polite to stoop slightly. Standing with hands on hips is considered arrogant. Blowing your nose in public is considered impolite, although burping isn't.

USEFUL EVERYDAY PHRASES

Yes
Ya

No
Bukan; tidak

There are two words that mean 'no' when replying to a
question in Indonesian. **Bukan** is used when the negative
relates to a noun and **tidak** is used when the negative relates to
an adjective, a preposition or a verb. For example, 'Is that your
car?' 'No, it isn't': **Apa itu mobil anda? Bukan. Itu bukan
mobil saya**; 'Do you want coffee, sir?' 'No, thank you': **Apa
Tuan mau minum kopi? Tidak, terima kasih**.

Thank you
Terima kasih

No, thank you
Tidak, terima kasih

Please *(requesting)*
Tolong

(offering)
Silakan

Yes, please
Ya, terima kasih

I don't understand
Saya tidak mengerti

Do you speak English/French/German?
Apa anda bicara bahasa Inggeris/Perancis/Jerman?

I can't speak Indonesian
Saya tidak dapat bicara bahasa Indonesia

I don't know
Saya tidak tahu

Please speak more slowly
Tolong bicara lebih pelan

Please write it down for me
Tolong tulis untuk saya

My name is …
Nama saya …

Good morning
Selamat pagi

Good afternoon *(from about 12.00 to about 15.00)*
Selamat siang

(from about 15.00 to about 18.00)
Selamat sore

Good evening/good night
Selamat malam

Goodbye
sampai jumpa lagi

---

ai *[I]*, au *[ow]*, c *[ch]*, e *[uh]*, e *[eh]*, i *[ee]*,
o *[hot]*, sy *[sh]*, u *[oo]*, v *[f]*; *see also pp5-6*

Goodbye *(said to person going on journey)*
Selamat jalan

(said by person going on journey)
Selamat tinggal

How are you?
Apa kabar?

Excuse me!
Maaf!

Pardon?
Maaf?

Sorry!
Maaf!

I'm really sorry!
Maaf sekali!

Can you help me?
Apa anda bisa tolong saya?

Can you tell me ...?
Boleh saya bertanya ...?

Can I have ...?
Boleh saya minta ...?

I would like ...
Saya ingin ...

Is there ... here?
Apa ada ... di sini?

Where can I get ...?
Di mana saya bisa dapatkan ...?

How much is it?
Berapa harganya?

What time is it?
Jam berapa?

I must go now
Saya harus pergi sekarang

I've lost my way
Saya kesasar

Cheers! *(toast)*
Selamat!

Do you take credit cards?
Apa anda terima kartu kredit?

Where is the toilet?
Di mana WC? *(weh seh)*

Go away!
Pergi!

Excellent!
Baik sekali!

---

ai *[I]*, au *[ow]*, c *[ch]*, e *[uh]*, e *[eh]*, i *[ee]*,
o *[hot]*, sy *[sh]*, u *[oo]*, v *[f]*; *see also pp5-6*

THINGS YOU'LL HEAR

ada apa?	what's the matter?
apa kabar?	how are you?
awas!	look out!
ayo	let's go; come on
baik, terima kasih	very well, thank you
– dan anda?	– and you?
ini	here you are
itu betul	that's right
maaf	excuse me
maaf?	pardon?
oh ya?	is that so?
sampai ketemu lagi	goodbye
sampai nanti	see you later
saya tidak mengerti	I don't understand
saya tidak tahu	I don't know
selamat datang!	welcome!
selamat jalan!	enjoy your trip!
selamat makan!	enjoy your meal!
silakan	go on; go ahead; help yourself
terima kasih	thanks
terima kasih kembali	you're welcome, don't mention it
tidak apa-apa	it doesn't matter
untuk apa?	what's the point?

THINGS YOU'LL SEE

air minum	drinking water
awas ...	beware of ...
buka	open
cat basah	wet paint
diisi	engaged
dijual	for sale

→

dilarang ...	no ..., do not ...
dilarang masuk	no admittance
dilarang merokok	no smoking
disewakan	for rent
dorong	push
harap tenang	silence please
harga mati	fixed price
jam buka	opening times
jam kunjungan	visiting hours
jangan ...	do not ...
jangan diganggu	do not disturb
kantor imigrasi	immigration office
kantor pariwisata	tourist information
kasa/kassa	till, cashier, pay here
keluar	way out
kosong	vacant
masuk	way in
masuk gratis	admission free
obral	sale
pintu darurat	emergency exit
pintu masuk	entrance
prangko	stamps
pria	gentlemen
pribadi	private
sudah dipesan	reserved
tarik	pull
tutup	closed
tutup selama libur	closed for holiday period
wanita	ladies

ai *[I]*, au *[ow]*, c *[ch]*, e *[uh]*, e̱ *[eh]*, i *[ee]*,
o *[hot]*, sy *[sh]*, u *[oo]*, v *[f]*; *see also pp5-6*

DAYS, MONTHS, SEASONS

Sunday	Minggu
Monday	Senin
Tuesday	Selasa
Wednesday	Rabu
Thursday	Kamis
Friday	Jumat
Saturday	Sabtu
January	Januari
February	Februari
March	Maret
April	April
May	Mei
June	Juni
July	Juli
August	Agustus
September	September
October	Oktober
November	November
December	Desember
Spring	Musim semi
Summer	Musim panas
Autumn	Musim gugur
Winter	Musim dingin
Christmas	Natal
Christmas Eve	Malam Natal
New Year	Tahun Baru
New Year's Eve	Malam Tahun Baru
Easter	Paskah
Good Friday	Jumat Besar

NUMBERS

0	nol	31	tiga puluh satu
1	satu	32	tiga puluh dua
2	dua	40	empat puluh
3	tiga	50	lima puluh
4	empat	60	enam puluh
5	lima	70	tujuh puluh
6	enam	80	delapan puluh
7	tujuh	90	sembilan puluh
8	delapan	100	seratus
9	sembilan	110	seratus sepuluh
10	sepuluh	200	dua ratus
11	sebelas	300	tiga ratus
12	dua belas	400	empat ratus
13	tiga belas	500	lima ratus
14	empat belas	600	enam ratus
15	lima belas	700	tujuh ratus
16	enam belas	800	delapan ratus
17	tujuh belas	900	sembilan ratus
18	delapan belas	1,000	seribu
19	sembilan belas	10,000	sepuluh ribu
20	dua puluh	20,000	dua puluh ribu
21	dua puluh satu	100,000	seratus ribu
22	dua puluh dua	1,000,000	sejuta
30	tiga puluh		

THE CALENDAR

The date is expressed by the word **tanggal** (date) followed by the relevant number and the month, for example:

3rd May	tanggal tiga Mei
20th June	tanggal dua puluh Juni

---

ai *[I]*, au *[ow]*, c *[ch]*, e *[uh]*, e̱ *[eh]*, i *[ee]*,
o *[hot]*, sy *[sh]*, u *[oo]*, v *[f]*; *see also pp5-6*

TIME

today	hari ini
yesterday	kemarin
tomorrow	besok
the day before yesterday	kemarin dulu
the day after tomorrow	lusa
this week	minggu ini
last week	minggu lalu
next week	minggu depan
this morning *(now)*	pagi ini
(time past)	pagi tadi
this afternoon *(now)*	sore ini
(time past)	sore tadi
this evening, tonight	malam ini
yesterday afternoon	kemarin sore
last night	tadi malam
tomorrow morning	besok pagi
tomorrow night	besok malam
in three days' time	tiga hari lagi
three days ago	tiga hari lalu
late	terlambat
early	pagi
soon	segera
later on	nanti
at the moment	saat ini
second	detik
minute	menit
one minute	satu menit
two minutes	dua menit
quarter of an hour	seperempat jam
half an hour	setengah jam
three quarters of an hour	tiga perempat jam
hour	jam
day	hari
that day	hari itu

every day	tiap hari
all day	seharian
the next day	hari berikut
week	minggu
month	bulan
year	tahun

TELLING THE TIME

'What time is it?' is **jam berapa?** or **pukul berapa?**. 'O'clock' is translated by **jam** or **pukul**, the Indonesian words for 'hour' and 'strike' respectively. '(It's) one o'clock' is **jam satu** or **pukul satu**; '(it's) four o'clock' is **jam empat** or **pukul empat** and so on.

To express minutes past the hour, use the word **lebih**, which means 'more', for example 'ten past five' is **jam lima lebih sepuluh**. For minutes to the hour use **kurang**, which means 'less', for example 'twenty to eleven' is **jam sebelas kurang dua puluh**.

'Quarter' is **seperempat**, so 'quarter past three' is **jam tiga lebih seperempat**, and 'quarter to eight' is **jam delapan kurang seperempat**.

'Half' is **setengah**, so 'half past five' is **setengah enam** literally 'half of six'.

The word 'at' in phrases such as 'at 2.15' can be translated by **pada**: **pada jam dua lebih seperempat**. However, **pada** is usually omitted in speech.

The expressions 'am' and 'pm' have no exact equivalents but the words **pagi** 'morning', **siang** 'midday', **sore** 'afternoon', and **malam** 'evening' or 'night' are used to distinguish between times that might otherwise be confused. For example, '5am' is **jam lima pagi** and '5pm' is **jam lima sore**; '7am' is **jam tujuh pagi** and '7pm' is **jam tujuh malam**; '11am' is **jam sebelas siang** and '11pm' is **jam sebelas malam**. Finally, **tengah hari** is 'midday' and **tengah malam** is 'midnight'.

---

ai *[I]*, au *[ow]*, c *[ch]*, e *[uh]*, e̱ *[eh]*, i *[ee]*, o *[hot]*, sy *[sh]*, u *[oo]*, v *[f]*; *see also pp5-6*

am	pagi
pm *(from about 12.00 to about 15.00)*	siang
(from about 15.00 to about 18.00)	sore
(from about 18.00 to midnight)	malam
one o'clock	jam satu
ten past one	jam satu lebih sepuluh
quarter past one	jam satu lebih seperempat
half past one	setengah dua
twenty to two	jam dua kurang dua puluh
quarter to two	jam dua kurang seperempat
two o'clock	jam dua
13.00	jam tiga belas
16.30	jam enam belas tiga puluh
at half past five	pada jam setengah enam
at seven o'clock	pada jam tujuh
noon	tengah hari
midnight	tengah malam

HOTELS

The most expensive and luxurious establishments of international standard can be found in Jakarta, on Bali and in a few large towns. There are also many comfortable hotels which aren't quite so luxurious. Most common are the moderately priced smaller establishments, often called **wisma** or **guesthouse** (pronounced *guesshouse*), and even cheaper, but still clean and comfortable, places known as **losmen** or **penginapan**.

Facilities range from air-conditioning, hot and cold water, Western-style toilets, and international cuisine at the expensive end of the market to a fan, cold water only, squatting toilets and local cuisine at the cheaper end.

Full-board and half-board terms are not available. The charge is for the room only and the cost of any meals and services such as laundry and telephone calls are added. In any hotel or **wisma** you can have any meal provided at more or less any time of day, but in the smaller establishments the meal may not be cooked on the premises but fetched from a nearby restaurant. The smaller the hotel the less there is in the way of public rooms like bars, dining rooms, lounges, and facilities like shops and swimming pools. In the simpler places you just have bedrooms round a courtyard, with either en suite or communal bathrooms and toilets. Credit cards are accepted in the larger hotels.

USEFUL WORDS AND PHRASES

air conditioning	AC (*ah seh*)
balcony	balkon
bathroom	kamar mandi
bed	tempat tidur
bedroom	kamar tidur
bill	bon, rekening

ai *[I]*, au *[ow]*, c *[ch]*, e *[uh]*, e *[eh]*, i *[ee]*, o *[hot]*, sy *[sh]*, u *[oo]*, v *[f]*; see also pp5-6

breakfast	makan pagi, sarapan
dining room	ruang makan, kamar makan
dinner	makan malam
double room	kamar untuk dua orang
foyer	ruang tunggu
hotel	hotel
key	kunci
lift	lift
lounge	ruang duduk
lunch	makan siang
manager	manajer
reception	penerimaan tamu
receptionist	penerima tamu
restaurant	restoran
room	kamar
room service	pelayanan kamar
shower	dus
single room	kamar untuk satu orang
toilet	wc *(weh seh)*
twin room	kamar dengan dua tempat tidur

Do you have any vacancies?
Apa ada kamar kosong?

I have a reservation
Saya sudah pesan

I'd like a single room
Saya mau kamar untuk satu orang

I'd like a double room
Saya mau kamar untuk dua orang

I'd like a twin room
Saya mau kamar dengan dua tempat tidur

I'd like a room with a bathroom/balcony
Saya mau kamar dengan kamar mandi/balkon

I'd like a room for one night/three nights
Saya mau kamar untuk satu malam/tiga malam

What is the charge per night?
Berapa sewanya satu malam?

I don't know yet how long I'll stay
Saya belum tahu berapa lama saya akan tinggal

When is breakfast/dinner?
Kapan makan pagi/makan malam?

Would you have my luggage brought up?
Tolong bawakan kopor saya ke kamar saya

Please wake me at six o'clock
Tolong bangunkan saya jam enam

Can I have breakfast in my room?
Dapat saya makan pagi di kamar saya?

I'll be back at ten o'clock
Saya akan kembali jam sepuluh

My room number is (205)
Kamar saya nomor (dua nol lima)

I need a light bulb
Saya perlu bola lampu

---

ai *[I]*, au *[ow]*, c *[ch]*, e *[uh]*, e̲ *[eh]*, i *[ee]*,
o *[hot]*, sy *[sh]*, u *[oo]*, v *[f]*; *see also pp5-6*

There is no toilet paper in the bathroom
Tidak ada kertas toilet di kamar mandi

The window won't open
Jendela macet

The lift/shower doesn't work
Lift/dus rusak

There isn't any hot water
Tidak ada air panas

There's no water
Tidak ada air

The socket in the bathroom doesn't work
Stopkontak di kamar mandi rusak

I'm leaving tomorrow
Saya berangkat besok

Can I have the bill, please?
Boleh minta rekeningnya?

I'll pay by credit card
Saya akan membayar dengan kartu kredit

I'll pay cash
Saya akan bayar kontan

Can you get me a taxi?
Dapat anda panggil taksi untuk saya?

Can you recommend another hotel?
Dapat anda sarankan hotel lain?

Things You'll See

AC	air conditioning
dorong	push
dus	shower
kamar makan	dining room
kamar mandi	bathroom
kamar untuk dua orang	double room
kamar untuk satu orang	single room
keluar	out
kolam renang	swimming pool
lantai dasar	ground floor
lantai dua	second floor
lantai satu	first floor
losmen	guesthouse
makan malam	evening meal
makan pagi	breakfast
makan siang	lunch
masuk	in
penginapan	guesthouse
penerimaan tamu	reception
penuh	no vacancies
pintu darurat	emergency exit
pria	gentlemen
rekening	bill
restoran	restaurant
ruang makan	dining room
sarapan	breakfast
tarik	pull
toko	shop
wanita	ladies
wisma	guesthouse

ai *[I]*, au *[ow]*, c *[ch]*, e *[uh]*, e̲ *[eh]*, i *[ee]*,
o *[hot]*, sy *[sh]*, u *[oo]*, v *[f]*; *see also pp5-6*

THINGS YOU'LL HEAR

Maaf, sudah penuh
I'm sorry, we're full

Kamar untuk satu orang sudah habis
There are no single rooms left

Kamar untuk dua orang sudah habis
There are no double rooms left

Untuk berapa malam?
For how many nights?

Bagaimana anda membayar?
How will you be paying?

Tolong bayar di muka
Please pay in advance

Anda mau kamar yang lebih murah?
Would you like a cheaper room?

Tolong paspornya
Your passport, please

Silakan isi formulir ini
Please fill in this form

MOTORING

Roads vary greatly in quality. There are a few motorways,
mainly in Java. They are called **jalan tol** (literally, 'toll roads')
because they all have toll-gates. The main roads are busy much
of the time, mostly with lorries and buses. Only a small
proportion of the population own private cars, although quite
a large percentage own motorbikes. A good many rugged Jeep-
like vehicles are used because they withstand the rough roads
better than ordinary cars.

The rule of the road is that drivers keep to the left, but
whether on crowded city streets or country roads driving is not
always an orderly affair, and is complicated by the large
numbers of motorbikes, the lack of pavements, and by chickens
and other animals on the roads, especially in the country.

In some tourist areas it is possible to hire a motorbike or self-
drive car, but for a sight-seeing trip taking in a number of
places, it is safer to hire a car with a driver. Generally, you are
advised not to try driving yourself. Whether you are in a city
like Jakarta, where the traffic can be very heavy and chaotic, or
in a country area, it is better (and not expensive by Western
standards) to hire a car with a driver who will be used to the
ways of local motorists and pedestrians, and will know where
to park and how to cope with accidents and other
emergencies. Few Indonesian drivers are insured so accidents
can have complicated consequences.

SOME COMMON ROAD SIGNS

akhir jalan tol	end of motorway
asrama tentara	military barracks
awas!	caution!
awas kereta api	beware of the trains

→

---

ai *[I]*, au *[ow]*, c *[ch]*, e *[uh]*, e̱ *[eh]*, i *[ee]*,
o *[hot]*, sy *[sh]*, u *[oo]*, v *[f]*; *see also pp5-6*

bahaya	danger
belokan berbahaya	dangerous bend
beri jalan	give way
dilarang berhenti	no stopping
dilarang masuk	no entry; no trespassing
dilarang melambung	no overtaking
dilarang parkir	no parking
hati-hati	caution
jalan buntu	dead end
jalan licin	slippery surface
jalan satu arah	one-way street
jalan tol	motorway with toll
mesjid	mosque
pejalan kaki	pedestrians
pejalan kaki jalan sebelah kiri	pedestrians keep to the left
perbaikan jalan	roadworks
perlahan-lahan	slow
persimpangan berbahaya	dangerous junction
PPPK	first aid
pusat kota	town centre
rumah sakit	hospital
sekolah	school
tempat parkir	car park
untuk kendaraan berat	for heavy vehicles
untuk mobil dinas	for official cars

USEFUL WORDS AND PHRASES

automatic	mobil persneling otomatis
boot	tempat bagasi
brake *(noun)*	rem
break down	mogok
car	mobil
car park	tempat parkir
clutch	kopling

drive *(verb)*	mengemudi
engine	mesin
exhaust	knalpot
fanbelt	tali kipas
garage *(for repairs)*	bengkel
(for petrol)	pompa bensin
gear	persneling
gears	gigi
headlights	lampu depan
licence	SIM *(seem)*
lorry	truk
manual	mobil persneling biasa
mirror	kaca spion
motorbike	sepeda motor
motorway	jalan tol
number plate	pelat nomor
petrol	bensin
rear lights	lampu belakang
road	jalan
spares	suku cadang
speed *(noun)*	kecepatan
speedometer	spedometer
steering wheel	setir
tow *(verb)*	menarik
traffic lights	lampu lalu-lintas
trailer	truk gandengan
tyre	ban
van	pikap tertutup
wheel	roda
windscreen	kaca depan
windscreen wiper	kipas kaca

I'd like some petrol/oil/water
Saya perlu bensin/oli/air

ai *[I]*, au *[ow]*, c *[ch]*, e *[uh]*, e *[eh]*, i *[ee]*,
o *[hot]*, sy *[sh]*, u *[oo]*, v *[f]*; *see also pp5-6*

Fill her up, please!
Tolong isi!

I'd like 35 litres of petrol
Saya perlu tiga puluh lima liter bensin

Would you check the tyres, please?
Tolong periksa ban

Do you do repairs?
Apa anda mengerjakan reparasi?

Can you repair the clutch?
Dapat anda memperbaiki kopling?

How long will it take?
Berapa lama selesainya?

Where can I park?
Di mana saya parkir mobil?

Can I park here?
Boleh saya parkir di sini?

There is something wrong with the engine
Ada yang tidak beres dengan mesin

The engine is overheating
Mesin kepanasan

I need a new tyre
Saya perlu ban baru

I'd like to hire a car
Saya mau menyewa mobil

For one day/two days/a week
Untuk satu hari/dua hari/satu minggu

Is there a mileage charge?
Apa jarak dipungut bayaran?

Where is the nearest garage?
Di mana bengkel terdekat?

How do I get to Ubud?
Bagaimana saya pergi ke Ubud?

Is this the road to Arau?
Apa ini jalan ke Arau?

THINGS YOU'LL SEE

antri	queue
bengkel mobil	car repairs
bensin	petrol
jalur lambat	crawler lane
keluar	exit
oli	oil
pompa bensin	petrol station
reparasi	repairs
solar	diesel fuel
tambal ban	tyre repairs
tekanan ban	tyre pressure
tekanan udara	air pressure
tempat servis mobil	service station

---

ai *[I]*, au *[ow]*, c *[ch]*, e *[uh]*, e̱ *[eh]*, i *[ee]*,
o *[hot]*, sy *[sh]*, u *[oo]*, v *[f]*; *see also pp5-6*

DIRECTIONS YOU MAY BE GIVEN

belok kanan	turn right
belok kiri	turn left
di kanan	on the right
di kiri	on the left
lewat ...	past the ...
lurus	straight on
yang kedua di kiri	second on the left
yang pertama di kanan	first on the right

THINGS YOU'LL HEAR

Apa anda mau mobil persneling otomatis atau mobil persneing biasa?
Would you like an automatic or a manual?

Boleh saya lihat SIM anda?
May I see your licence?

Apa anda punya SIM Indonesia atau internasional?
Do you hold an Indonesian or international licence?

Di mana SIM anda dikeluarkan?
Where was your licence issued?

Berapa liter?
How many litres?

Apa anda perlu oli?
Do you need oil?

TRAVELLING AROUND

AIR TRAVEL

Indonesia is served by most major international airlines and has several international airports: they include Jakarta, Solo and Surabaya on the island of Java; Denpasar in Bali; Jayapura in Irian Jaya; Medan and Pekan Baru in Sumatra; and Menado in Sulawesi.

Indonesia's main international airline is Garuda, the other is Sempati. A network of domestic routes is flown by the state-owned Garuda and Merpati, and also by the privately-run companies Sempati, Bouraq and Mandala. Small airports are called **lapangan terbang** and large airports **bandar udara**. There are fewer facilities such as shops and restaurants in the smaller airports. Waiting rooms are smaller and there will be fewer taxis available.

SEA TRAVEL

A more leisurely way to travel between the main islands of Indonesia is on one of the large ocean-going ferries run by Pelni, the national shipping company. The ships are modern and comfortable and offer a cheaper, if slower, way of travelling than flying. Routes extend from north Sumatra in the west to Irian Jaya in the east.

RAIL TRAVEL

Nearly all the cities in Java and some in Sumatra are served by the state-owned railway. Long-distance expresses with sleepers (four beds to a compartment) link Jakarta with Surabaya. Some overnight trains simply have reclining seats. Seats are all very reasonably priced by Western standards. They should be booked 24 hours in advance, either at the station or through a travel agent.

---

ai *[I]*, au *[ow]*, c *[ch]*, e *[uh]*, e̲ *[eh]*, i *[ee]*, o *[hot]*, sy *[sh]*, u *[oo]*, v *[f]*; *see also pp5-6*

BUSES

Buses are the cheapest and commonest means of public
transport in most of Indonesia. Long-distance buses, often air-
conditioned, and minibuses ply between towns and cities; you
can even travel on the same bus from north Sumatra as far as
Bali – a distance of over 1,000 miles. Within towns, a variety
of buses, minibuses and even smaller vehicles (called **mikrolet**,
oplet, **bemo**) seating about six provide a frequent service and
usually operate at a standard fare for any journey.

TAXIS AND OTHER TRANSPORT

In most large towns there are taxis which you can book to
pick you up from a given point, and in some towns **bajaj**
(motorised tricycles) seating two or three passengers can be
hired. At busy times of day or on public holidays when buses
are literally crammed full, for relatively long journeys (such
as the 2hr 45m drive from Jakarta to Bandung) a shared taxi
can be hired quite cheaply. You either book in advance or
wait at the taxi office until enough people want to go to the
same place.

For short trips the traditional **becak** (trishaw) is often used.
A variety of horse-drawn buggies (called **delman**, **sado**,
andong, **bendi**) are also to be found in areas where motor
traffic is not too heavy. It is customary to agree a price
beforehand with the driver. Ask 'How much is it to …?' **Berapa
ke …?** When the driver has named a price, you should offer
half of it but finally agree on a sum in between.

USEFUL WORDS AND PHRASES

airport (*large*)	bandar udara
(*small*)	lapangan terbang
airport bus	bis bandar udara
aisle seat	kursi dekat gang
adult	dewasa
baggage claim	pengambilan barang, kopor

boarding card	kartu naik pesawat
boat	kapal
booking office	kantor buking
buffet	bufet
bus	bis
bus station	terminal bis *(tairmeenal)*
bus stop	perhentian bis
carriage *(train)*	gerbong
change *(verb)*	ganti
check-in desk	tempat cek in
child	anak
coach *(bus)*	bis
compartment	kompartemen
connection	sambungan
Customs	bea cukai
departure lounge	ruang keberangkatan
domestic	domestik
domestic arrivals	kedatangan domestik
domestic departures	keberangkatan domestik
emergency exit	pintu darurat
entrance	masuk
exit	keluar
fare	harga karcis, ongkos perjalanan
ferry	feri
first class	kelas satu
flight	penerbangan
flight number	nomor penerbangan
gate	pintu
hand luggage	barang tentengan
international	internasional
international arrivals	kedatangan internasional
international departures	keberangkatan internasional
left luggage office	tempat penyimpanan barang

ai *[I]*, au *[ow]*, c *[ch]*, e *[uh]*, e *[eh]*, i *[ee]*,
o *[hot]*, sy *[sh]*, u *[oo]*, v *[f]*; *see also pp5-6*

lost property office	tempat barang hilang
luggage trolley	kereta dorong untuk barang
network map	peta jaringan kereta api
non-smoking	tidak merokok
number 5 bus	bis nomor 5
passport	paspor
platform	peron
port	pelabuhan
quay	dermaga
railway	kereta api
reserved seat	kursi pesanan
restaurant car	restorasi
return ticket	karcis pergi pulang
sea	laut
seat	kursi
second class	kelas dua
ship	kapal
single ticket	karcis satu jalan
sleeper	kursi tidur
smoking	merokok
station	stasiun
taxi	taksi
terminus *(bus)*	terminal bis *(tairmeenal)*
ticket *(air)*	tiket
(bus, rail)	karcis
timetable	jadwal
train	kereta api
visa	visa *(fee-sah)*
waiting room	ruang tunggu
window seat	kursi dekat jendela

AIR TRAVEL

I'd like a non-smoking seat, please
Saya mau kursi di tempat tidak merokok

I'd like a window seat, please
Saya mau kursi dekat jendela

How long will the flight be delayed?
Berapa lama penerbangan akan terlambat?

Which gate for the flight to Medan?
Pintu mana untuk penerbangan ke Medan?

Bus, Rail and Ferry Travel

When does the train/bus for Bandung leave?
Kapan kereta api/bis untuk Bandung berangkat?

When does the train/bus from Semarang arrive?
Kapan kereta api/bis dari Semarang tiba?

When is the next train/bus to Surabaya?
Kapan kereta api/bis berikutnya ke Surabaya?

When is the first train/bus to Jakarta?
Kapan kereta api/bis pertama ke Jakarta?

When is the last train/bus to Cirebon?
Kapan kereta api/bis terakhir ke Cirebon?

What is the fare to Bukittinggi?
Berapa harga karcis ke Bukittinggi?

Do I have to change?
Apa saya harus ganti kereta api?

---

ai *[I]*, au *[ow]*, c *[ch]*, e *[uh]*, e *[eh]*, i *[ee]*,
o *[hot]*, sy *[sh]*, u *[oo]*, v *[f]*; *see also pp5-6*

Does the train/bus stop at Pekalongan?
Apa kereta api/bis berhenti di Pekalongan?

How long does it take to get to Borobudur?
Berapa lama ke Borobudur?

Where can I buy a ticket?
Di mana saya dapat beli karcis?

A single/return ticket to Denpasar, please
Karcis satu jalan/pergi-pulang ke Denpasar

Could you help me get a ticket?
Dapat anda bantu saya mendapatkan karcis?

Do I have to pay a supplement?
Apa saya harus membayar tuslah?

I'd like to reserve a seat
Saya mau pesan tempat

Is this the right train/bus for Bandung?
Apa ini kereta api/bis yang betul untuk Bandung?

Is this the right platform for the Bogor train?
Apa ini peron yang betul untuk kereta api ke Bogor?

Which platform for the Madiun train?
Peron mana untuk kereta api ke Madiun?

Is the train/bus late?
Apa kereta api/bis terlambat?

Could you help me with my luggage, please?
Dapat anda bantu saya dengan barang saya?

Is this a non-smoking compartment?
Apa ini kompartemen tidak merokok?

Is this seat free?
Apa kursi ini kosong?

This seat is taken
Kursi ini sudah diisi

I have reserved this seat
Saya sudah pesan kursi ini

May I open/close the window?
Boleh saya buka/tutup jendela?

When do we arrive in Ujung Pandang?
Kapan kita tiba di Ujung Pandang?

What station is this?
Stasiun apa ini?

Do we stop at Tegal?
Apa kita berhenti di Tegal?

Would you keep an eye on my things for a moment?
Bisa anda jaga barang-barang saya sebentar?

Is there a restaurant car on this train?
Apa ada gerbong restorasi di kereta api ini?

---

ai *[I]*, au *[ow]*, c *[ch]*, e *[uh]*, e *[eh]*, i *[ee]*,
o *[hot]*, sy *[sh]*, u *[oo]*, v *[f]*; *see also pp5-6*

Where is the bus station?
Di mana terminal bis? *(tairmeenal)*

Where is there a bus stop?
Di mana perhentian bis?

Which buses go to Limau Manis?
Bis mana ke Limau Manis?

How often do the buses to Suliki run?
Berapa sering bis ke Suliki?

Will you let me know when we're there?
Dapat anda beritahu saya bila kita sampai di sana?

Do I have to get off yet?
Apa saya harus turun?

How do you get to Pasar Ikan?
Bagaimana kita pergi ke Pasar Ikan?

Do you go near Prambanan?
Apa anda pergi dekat Prambanan?

Where can I get a ferry to Pulau Samosir?
Di mana saya bisa naik feri ke Pulau Samosir?

TAXI, BECAK ETC

I want to go to Banda Aceh
Saya mau pergi ke Banda Aceh

How much is it to the station?
Berapa ke stasiun?

I'll give you 2000 rupiah
Dua ribu rupiah, ya?

Agreed
Baiklah

Can you let me off here?
Stop di sini

Could you wait here for me and take me back?
Bisa tunggu di sini dan antarkan saya kembali?

THINGS YOU'LL SEE

anak-anak	children
bis	buses
dewasa	adults
diharap tidak merokok	no smoking, please
dilarang bicara dengan pengemudi	do not speak to the driver
dilarang masuk	no entry
dilarang mengeluarkan anggota badan	do not lean out of the window
dilarang merokok	no smoking
feri	ferry
gerbong	carriage
hari Minggu dan hari besar	Sundays and public holidays
informasi	information
jadwal	timetable
karcis	ticket
keberangkatan	departure
kecuali hari Minggu	Sundays excepted ⟶

---

ai *[I]*, au *[ow]*, c *[ch]*, e *[uh]*, e̲ *[eh]*, i *[ee]*,
o *[hot]*, sy *[sh]*, u *[oo]*, v *[f]*; *see also pp5-6*

kedatangan	arrivals
ke kereta api	to the trains
keluar	way out, exit
kios	newspaper kiosk
loket	ticket office
makanan ringan	snacks
masuk	entrance
masuk dari pintu depan/belakang	entry at the front/rear
pelabuhan	harbour
pemeriksaan bea cukai	customs control
penerangan	information
penerbangan	flight
penerbangan biasa	scheduled flight
penerbangan domestik	domestic flights
penerbangan internasional	international flights
penerbangan langsung	direct flight
pengambilan barang	baggage claim
perhentian bis	bus stop
peron	platform
pintu darurat	emergency exit
pintu embarkasi	gate
PJKA	Indonesian State Railways
ruang tunggu	waiting room
rute	route
stasiun	station
taksi	taxi
tempat penyimpanan barang	left luggage
terlambat	delay
terminal	terminus
terminal bis	bus station
tuslah	supplement
waktu setempat	local time
wc pria	gents
wc wanita	ladies

REPLIES YOU MAY BE GIVEN

Kereta api berikut berangkat jam satu
The next train leaves at one o'clock

Ganti di Surabaya
Change at Surabaya

Anda harus bayar tuslah
You must pay a supplement

Tempat untuk Bandung sudah habis
There are no more seats available for Bandung

THINGS YOU'LL HEAR

Tidak berhenti di Rembang
Does not stop in Rembang

Para penumpang penerbangan ke London dipersilakan naik pesawat
The flight for London is now boarding

Para penumpang dipersilakan menuju pintu nomor tiga
Please go now to gate number three

Perhatian!
Attention!

Naik kereta api
Board the train

Kereta api ke Bandung akan berangkat dari peron nomor satu dalam waktu sepuluh menit
The train for Bandung will leave from platform one in ten minutes

→

ai *[I]*, au *[ow]*, c *[ch]*, e *[uh]*, e̱ *[eh]*, i *[ee]*,
o *[hot]*, sy *[sh]*, u *[oo]*, v *[f]*; see also pp5-6

Kereta api ke Jakarta akan tiba di peron nomor dua dalam waktu lima menit
The train for Jakarta will arrive at platform two in five minutes

Kereta api ke Jakarta terlambat lima belas menit
The train for Jakarta is running fifteen minutes late

Tolong siapkan karcisnya
Tickets ready, please

Tolong paspornya
Your passport, please

Tolong buka kopor anda
Open your suitcases, please

Ada barang yang harus anda laporkan?
Do you have anything to declare?

RESTAURANTS

Indonesian food varies quite considerably from region to region. For example, food in central Java is rather sweet and mild, a typical dish being **nasi gudeg** – rice with jackfruit and coconut milk. By contrast, West Sumatran (Padang) food has a reputation for being very hot and spicy; try a famous local dish like rendang – spiced coconut beef – and you'll notice the difference! Restaurants selling local food are in every town, and most larger towns will have Chinese restaurants. As most Indonesians are Muslims, it is only in these that you'll find pork dishes. However, in spite of religious considerations, bottled beer is sold readily in most restaurants. In international hotels and in restaurants located in the busy tourist centres such as Yogyakarta and Bali, European and American-style food is available.

Rice is the staple food of the Indonesian diet – for breakfast, lunch and evening meal. A typical meal consists of boiled rice, **nasi putih**, accompanied by chicken, fish, beef and vegetables with hot, pungent condiments, and rounded off with bananas, papaya, mango (good for cooling a mouth burnt by chillis) and other fruit. Traditionally, fried rice, **nasi goreng**, is eaten for breakfast, making use of any cooked rice and other food left over from the day before, although it is now a speciality in its own right. Meals are usually served with rice and hot tea without milk or boiled water. Indonesians eat with their hands (right hand only) or with a fork and spoon.

If you feel you can cope with hot spicy food, look out for West Sumatran restaurants, **rumah makan Padang**, which are in most large towns. You don't have to order food in a **rumah makan Padang** restaurant. Sit down and the waiter will fill your table with anything from ten to twenty small dishes, each containing a different speciality of the region. Then just help yourself, taking a little at a time, sharing it with your friends.

---

ai *[I]*, au *[ow]*, c *[ch]*, e *[uh]*, ę *[eh]*, i *[ee]*,
o *[hot]*, sy *[sh]*, u *[oo]*, v *[f]*; *see also pp5-6*

When you've finished, the waiter will total up your bill according to what you've taken.

Tea and coffee are usually served without milk and very sweet. Bear in mind that if you ask for milk, it will probably be tinned condensed milk, rendering your drink even sweeter. A mouth-watering variety of fruit and fruit juices are available, although juices, including avocado and tomato juice, will also be served with lots of sugar.

Tipping is not customary in Indonesia, though you might be expected to tip in large international hotels.

From roadside stalls, **warung**, and itinerant food-sellers you can buy a wide variety of dishes, such as **sate** (small pieces of barbecued meat on a skewer with peanut or soy sauce and chilli relish), **bakso** (meatball soup), **ketoprak** (salad and fried tofu with peanut sauce), noodles, cakes and fruit. The night time provides the best opportunity for relaxing over a delicious meal in the open when the glaring heat of the sun has gone. Watch the stalls selling clothes, shoes, buckets, pans and watches during the day shut down as night falls, only to be replaced by **warung** after **warung** selling a wide variety of local dishes.

USEFUL WORDS AND PHRASES

beer	bir
bill	bon, rekening
black coffee, no sugar	kopi pahit
black tea, no sugar	teh pahit
bottle	botol
bowl	mangkuk
bread	roti
chopsticks	supit
coffee	kopi
coffee with milk	kopi susu
cup	cangkir
fork	garpu
glass	gelas
knife	pisau

menu	menu *(menoo)*
milk	susu
plate	piring
receipt	kwitansi
restaurant	restoran
salt	garam
serviette	serbet
snack	makanan kecil
soup	sup
spoon	sendok
sugar	gula
tea	teh
tea with milk	teh susu
teaspoon	sendok teh
tip	'tip'
waiter	pelayan
waitress	pelayan wanita
water	air putih
wine	anggur
wine list	daftar anggur

A table for one/two, please
Meja untuk satu/dua orang

Can I see the menu/wine list?
Boleh saya lihat menu/daftar anggur? *(menoo)*

What would you recommend?
Apa anda anjurkan?

I'd like ...
Saya mau ...

---

ai *[I]*, au *[ow]*, c *[ch]*, e *[uh]*, e *[eh]*, i *[ee]*,
o *[hot]*, sy *[sh]*, u *[oo]*, v *[f]*; *see also pp5-6*

Not too hot (spicy), OK?
Jangan terlalu pedas, ya?

Is it very hot (spicy)?
Apa itu pedas sekali?

I can't eat hot (spicy) food
Saya tak bisa makan pedas

Is there any food without meat or chicken?
Ada makanan yang tidak pakai daging atau ayam?

Could I have a glass of water, please?
Minta segelas air putih

Just a cup of coffee, please
Saya mau satu cangkir kopi saja

A glass of tomato juice without sugar
Segelas air tomat yang tidak pakai gula

Waiter! *(younger)*	*(older)*
dik!/bung!	mas!/pak!

Waitress! *(younger)*	*(older)*
dik!/nona!	mbak!/bu!

Can we have the bill, please?
Tolong bon

I only want a snack
Saya hanya mau makanan ringan

I didn't order this
Saya tidak pesan ini

May we have some more …?
Boleh kami minta lagi …?

The meal was very good, thank you
Makanannya sangat lezat, terima kasih

THINGS YOU MAY HEAR

Silakan masuk
Please come in

Silakan duduk
Please sit down

Berapa orang?
For how many?

Pesan apa?
What would you like?

Itu pedas
That's hot (spicy)

Anda suka makanan pedas?
Do you like hot (spicy) food?

Selamat makan!
Enjoy your meal!

Anda mau kopi?
Would you like coffee?

---

ai *[I]*, au *[ow]*, c *[ch]*, e *[uh]*, e̲ *[eh]*, i *[ee]*,
o *[hot]*, sy *[sh]*, u *[oo]*, v *[f]*; *see also pp5-6*

MENU GUIDE

abon	fried shredded beef
abon ayam	fried shredded chicken
acar bening	mixed vegetable pickle
acar campur	cooked vegetable salad
acar kuning	mixed vegetable pickle with turmeric
aduk-aduk tempe	stir-fried *tempe* and shrimps in coconut
air	water
air belimbing	star fruit juice
air jahe	ginger tea
air jeruk	orange juice; orangeade
air kelapa muda	young coconut juice
air mineral	mineral water
air nanas	pineapple juice
air putih	water
air sirop	fruit syrup
air sirsak	soursop juice
air tomat	tomato juice
anggur merah	red wine
anggur putih	white wine
angsa	goose
apel	apple
arbei	strawberry
arem-arem	steamed rice with beef and coconut
asam	tamarind; sour
asam manis	with sweet and sour sauce
asam pedas	hot and sour sauce
asem-asem kepiting	spicy crab
asin	salty, salted
asinan	pickled vegetables; pickled, salted
asinan bawang	pickled shallots
asinan campur	fruit and vegetable salad with vinegar and chilli dressing
asinan sayur	pickled vegetables
asinan wortel	pickled carrots
asin tahu	tofu and salted fish casserole
awuk-awuk	steamed red and white layer cake
ayam	chicken
ayam bakar	charcoal-grilled chicken
ayam goreng bumbu	fried spicy chicken

ayam goreng kalasan	fried chicken with garlic and coconut
ayam hijau	fried chicken with lemon grass and chillies
ayam kecap	chicken with spices and soy sauce
ayam kukus segar	steamed chicken with soy sauce and ginger
ayam panggang bumbu rujak	grilled spiced chicken
ayam panggang santan bumbu kecap	grilled chicken with coconut and soy sauce
ayam rica-rica	Manado-style grilled chicken with ginger
ayam tauco	chicken with yellow bean sauce
babat	tripe
babat goreng	fried tripe
babi	pork
babi giling	barbecued whole pig
babi panggang	barbecued pork
bacang	banana or bamboo leaf stuffed with rice and meat
bakar	baked, roast
bakmi	rice noodles
bakso	fish or meat balls
bakso daging	meat balls
bakso ikan	fish balls
bakso tahu	meat or fish balls with bean curd
bakwan	shrimp and beansprout fritters
bangkuang	yam-bean (similar to potato)
bawang	shallots
bawang bombay	onions
bawang daun	spring onions
bawang merah	shallots
bawang putih	garlic
bayam	type of spinach
belimbing	star fruit
beras	uncooked rice
besengek	meat stewed in coconut milk
bihun	rice noodles
bihun goreng	fried rice noodles
bihun kuah	rice-noodle soup
bir	beer, lager
bir Bintang®	Bintang beer®
bir hitam	dark beer

MENU GUIDE

bistik	steak
blewah	canteloupe melon
brem	rice wine (Balinese)
brongkos	fried beef in soy sauce
buah	fruit
buah anggur	grapes
buah ceri	cherries
bubur	rice porridge
bubur ayam	rice porridge with pieces of chicken, soy sauce, soya beans and shallots
bubur kacang hijau	porridge made from mung beans
bubur kedaton	vegetable stew with corn and *tempe*
bubur ketan	sticky-rice porridge
bubur Manado	Manado-style rice porridge served with vegetable soup or vegetables and fish
bumbu-bumbu	spices
bumbu kacang	peanut sauce
buncis	beans
bunga kol	cauliflower
buntil	cassava leaves with coconut and fish
buras	banana leaf stuffed with rice and steamed
cabe	chilli peppers
campur	mixed
capcai	stir-fried vegetables
cendawan	mushrooms
cengkeh	cloves
cenil	tapioca-flour rolls in grated coconut
cincang	chopped; minced
coklat panas	hot chocolate
coto Mangkasara	Sulawesi-style entrails and meat soup
cumi clorot	steamed stuffed squid
cumi-cumi	squid
cumi gulai kuning	squid stew with coconut, chilli and turmeric
cumi masak kecap	squid cooked in soy sauce
dadar gulung	pancakes filled with sweet coconut
dadar kuah	eggs and noodles in coconut sauce
daging	meat
daging asam	hot and sour beef
daging bungkus kol	cabbage rolls stuffed with beef
daging bebek	duck

daging rendang	meat cooked in coconut milk and spices until dry
daging sapi	beef
daging sapi cincang	minced beef
daun selada	lettuce
dendeng	dried, thin slices of beef
dendeng balado	beef dried with chillies and served in crisp, thin slices
dendeng semut	spicy thin slices of dried beef with grated coconut
domba	lamb
dodol	rice-flour dessert made with palm sugar
duku	small fruit similar to a lychee
durian	large, strong-smelling fruit with green spiky skin and yellow fine-tasting flesh
ebi	dried shrimps
empal pedas	fried beef with chillies
emping	bitter crisps made from crushed nuts
es	ice
es agar-agar	jelly with fruit syrup, coconut milk and ice
es cendol	drink made from droplets of rice flour in palm-sugar syrup and coconut milk with ice
es cincau	black vegetable jelly with fruit syrup, coconut milk and ice
es gandul	ball of crushed ice with fruit syrup
es jeruk	orange juice with ice
es kelapa	coconut milk with ice
es kelapa muda	young coconut drink with ice
es kopyor	coconut drink with ice
es krim	ice cream
es krim coklat	chocolate ice cream
es krim kelapa muda	coconut ice cream
es krim vanila	vanilla ice cream
es teler	tropical fruit salad with ice
gado-gado	vegetable salad with peanut sauce
gadon	steamed meatloaf in coconut milk
garam	salt
geplak	rice-flour cakes with coconut and sugar
getas	fried glutinous rice cakes in fruit syrup
getuk	cakes made from cassava

MENU GUIDE

giling	minced
ginjal	kidneys
goreng	fried
goreng ikan asin	fried salted fish
goreng limpa	fried cow's spleen
goreng oncom	fried *oncom*
goreng otak	fried brains
goreng pisang	fried banana, banana fritter
goreng ubi	fried tapioca; fried sweet potatoes
gula	sugar
gula jawa	coconut palm sugar
gulai	meat stewed in coconut milk
gulai kambing	goat's meat or mutton cooked in coconut milk
gulai otak	brains cooked in coconut milk
gulai parsanga	mutton curry
gulai udang merah	shrimps stewed in coconut milk
gula merah	coconut palm sugar
hati	liver
hati ayam masak jamur	chicken livers with mushrooms
ikan	fish
ikan air tawar	freshwater fish
ikan asin	salted fish
ikan basah	fresh fish
ikan bakar	charcoal-grilled fish
ikan bawal	pomfret (a local fish)
ikan belut	eel
ikan bumbu Bali	fish in a very hot, spicy sauce
ikan cuik	steamed, salted fish
ikan duri	catfish
ikan goreng	fried fish
ikan gurami	carp
ikan hiu	shark
ikan jolong-jolong	garfish
ikan kecap	fish in soy sauce
ikan laut	saltwater fish
ikan lele	catfish
ikan lemuru	sardine
ikan lidah	sole
ikan lindung	eel
ikan mas	carp

ikan mua	eel
ikan peda bungkus tahu	steamed tofu and salted fish
ikan sardin	sardine
ikan tenggiri	Spanish mackerel
ikan teri	small fish, usually anchovies
ikan tongkol	tuna fish
itik	duck
jadah	baked sticky rice-flour cake
jagung	sweet corn
jagung bakar	roasted sweet corn
jahe	ginger; ginger tea
jambu	rose-apple – red, pink or white heart-shaped fruit
jambu batu	guava – fruit with a green skin and sweet, pink flesh
jamur	mushrooms
jenang	palm-sugar and sticky rice cakes
jeruk	citrus fruit
jeruk asam	lemon
jeruk bali	pomelo
jeruk kepruk	tangerine
jeruk limau	lemon
jeruk manis	orange
jeruk nipis/jeruk purut	lime
jintan	cumin
kacang	peanuts
kacang hijau	mung beans
kacang panjang	runner beans
kalio	beef cooked in coconut milk and spices
kambing	goat
kangkung	water spinach
kangkung ca	stir-fried water spinach
kapurung	fish and vegetable soup with sago
karedok	raw vegetables with peanut sauce
kari	curry
kari ayam	curried chicken
kari otak	curried brains
kates	papaya – oblong fruit with yellow skin and orange flesh
kayu manis	cinnamon
kecap	soy sauce

MENU GUIDE

kecap asin	salty soy sauce
kecap manis	sweet soy sauce
kedondong	plum-shaped fruit with firm flesh and a single, spiny seed, with a flavour similar to cooking apples
keju	cheese
kelapa	coconut
kelepon	rice balls with palm-sugar centre coated with grated coconut
kencur	aromatic ginger
kentang	potato
kepiting	crab
kepiting pedas	crab in spicy sauce
kerang	clams
keripik tempe dan teri	crispy, fried *tempe* with dried anchovies
kerupuk	crackers
kerupuk ikan	fish crackers
kerupuk kulit	goat or cow-skin crackers
kerupuk udang	prawn crackers
ketan srikaya	steamed glutinous rice and coconut
ketimun	cucumber
ketoprak	mixed vegetables with fried tofu and peanut sauce
ketumbar	coriander
ketupat	banana leaf stuffed with compressed boiled rice
ketupat ketan	banana leaf stuffed with compressed boiled glutinous rice
kodok	frog
kol	cabbage
kolak	coconut syrup or fruit in coconut milk
kolak ubi	sweet potatoes in coconut syrup
kopi	coffee
kopi manis	coffee with sugar
kopi pahit	black coffee
kopi susu	coffee with milk
kotokan jambal	dried, salted fish curry
krim	cream
kue	cake, biscuit
kue bugis	small coconut cakes
kue cucur	rice-flour and palm-sugar cakes

kue ku	steamed glutinous rice and mung bean cakes
kue lapis	layer-cake flavoured with nutmeg
kue lumpang	steamed cakes with grated coconut
kue lumpur	coconut and raisin cake
kue mangkok	rice-flour, tapioca and coconut cake
kue pisang	rice cake with banana filling
kue pukis	small, thin crescent-shaped cake, sometimes with chocolate topping
kue sus	cake with custard filling
kue talam pisang	bananas in thick coconut-milk sauce
kue talam ubi	sweet potato and coconut cake
kue tar	tart
kue tarcis	small tart
kuitiau	noodles with meat and vegetables
kukus	steamed
kunyit	turmeric
kurma	dates
labu	pumpkin
lada merah	cayenne pepper; red chilli
laksa	rice-noodle soup made with coconut milk and spices
langsat	small fruit with brown skin and mildly acidic flavour
lemang	sticky rice cooked in hollowed-out bamboo over an open fire
lemper	banana leaf stuffed with sticky rice and meat
lengkeng	lychee
lengkuas	galingale – root used in savoury dishes
lidah panggang	barbecued beef tongue
limau	citrus fruit
limpa	spleen
limun	lemonade
loka anjoroe	boiled unripe banana served in thick coconut milk and eaten with dried fish
lombok	chilli
lombok rawit	small, very hot chilli
lomie	noodles in soy sauce, often with garlic, chilli and shallots
lontong	cubes or small cakes of boiled rice

lopis	sticky rice rolls
lotek	steamed or raw vegetables mixed with spicy peanut sauce
lumpia	spring rolls
madu	honey
madumongso	sticky rice with coconut and palm sugar
masakan daerah	regional specialities
makanan khas/khusus daerah	regional specialities
makanan pencuci mulut	fruit, desserts or sweets served at the end of a meal
makan malam	evening meal
makan pagi	breakfast
makan siang	lunch
mangga	mango
manggis	mangosteen – round fruit with thick reddish-brown skin (which stains the fingers) about the size of an apple with white juicy segments
manis	sweet
markisa	passion fruit
martabak	thick pancakes
masakan	cuisine
mentah	unripe; raw
mentega	butter
mentimun	cucumber
mentok singkong	savoury cassava pancakes
merica	black pepper
mie	noodles
mie bakso	noodles with fish or meat balls
mie bakso goreng	fried noodles with meat balls
mie bakso kuah	noodle soup with meat balls
mie goreng	fried noodles
mie rebus	noodles in soup
mihun	rice noodles
minyak	oil
mostar	mustard
mpe-mpe	fried pastry made from sago flour and fish, often with egg, vegetable or papaya filling and tamarind or chilli sauce
nagasari	rice cake with banana
nanas	pineapple

nangka	jackfruit – melon-shaped fruit with yellow flesh of a bread-like texture
nasi	cooked rice
nasi ayam	rice with chicken
nasi bumbu	rice with herbs
nasi campur	plain rice with meat and vegetable side dishes
nasi cemba	meat cooked with grated coconut and spices
nasi goreng	fried rice
nasi goreng babat	fried rice with tripe
nasi goreng bahari	fried rice with seafood
nasi goreng istimewa	special fried rice, usually with a fried egg, crackers and cucumber
nasi gudeg	rice with jackfruit and coconut milk
nasi gurih	rice cooked in coconut milk, served with various side dishes
nasi ketan	sticky rice
nasi kuning	yellow rice, sometimes served with meat or vegetable side dishes
nasi lemak	rice cooked in coconut milk
nasi liwet	boiled rice
nasi putih	boiled and steamed rice
nasi rames	rice with meat and vegetable side dishes
nasi soto	dish of rice served with meat soup
nasi uduk	rice cooked in coconut milk
oncom	fermented cake of soya bean sediment
onde-onde	sesame seed and mung bean balls
onde-onde wijen	fried ball of dough with a palm-sugar centre and a coating of sesame seeds
opor	meat cooked in coconut milk
opor ayam	chicken cooked in coconut milk
orak-arik kepiting	stir-fried crab with egg
oseng-oseng campur	stir-fried vegetables
oseng-oseng daging	stir-fried meat and vegetables
otak	brains
otak-otak	banana leaf stuffed with anchovies and coconut and cooked over an open fire
pala	nutmeg
pallu ce'la	fish cooked with spices until it is dry

pallu mara	sea fish cooked with coconut, tomato and chillies
pamplemus	grapefruit
panekuk	pancakes
pangek bungkus	steamed fish with spices
panggang	baked, grilled, roast
pangsit	boiled or steamed dumplings, usually containing minced meat and prawns
pangsit goreng	fried minced meat and prawn dumplings
papaya	fruit with yellow skin and soft, sweet orange flesh
paru	lungs
pastel	pie
pecai	Chinese cabbage
pecel	mixed steamed vegetables with hot peanut sauce
pecel lele	catfish with hot chillies
pedas	hot, spicy
penutup	desserts
pepes ayam	steamed chicken
pepes ikan	steamed fish
pepes jamur kuping	banana leaf stuffed with mushrooms and steamed
pergedel	potato cakes made with egg and spices
pergedel daging	potato cakes with minced beef
pergedel jagung	sweet corn fritters
perkedel	potato cakes made with egg and spices
perkedel kepiting	stuffed crabs
permen	sweets
petai	stink beans – similar to butter beans
petis	fish paste
pindang ikan	fish cooked slowly in spices
pindang telur	eggs cooked slowly in spices
pindang tongkol	tuna cooked slowly in spices
pisang	banana
pisang goreng	banana fritter
poding	pudding
putu mayang	steamed rice-flour cakes with coconut and palm-sugar sauce
putu tegal	steamed banana cakes with coconut and palm sugar

rambutan	small fruit like a lychee with reddish prickly skin and white flesh
rawon	diced beef cooked in a spicy black sauce
rebus	boiled
rempeyek	fritter made from peanuts or anchovies
rendang	meat cooked in coconut milk and spices until dry
roti	bread
roti tawar	unsweetened bread
rujak	hot, spicy fruit salad
rujak cingur	cooked vegetables mixed with peanut sauce and boiled cow's snout
rujak cuka	hot, spicy fruit salad with palm-sugar sauce
rujak kangkung	water spinach in spicy sauce
rujak ulek	thinly-sliced sweet potatoes and mixed tropical fruit with a dressing made from palm-sugar, tamarind and chilli
salak	pear-shaped fruit with white, dry, hard flesh and distinctive brown, snake-like scaly skin
sambal	hot chilli and shrimp-paste sauce
sambal goreng hati	pieces of liver cooked in *sambal*
sambal goreng hati dan tahu	liver and bean curd cooked in *sambal*
sambal goreng kentang	potatoes cooked in *sambal*
sambal goreng tempe	*tempe* cooked in *sambal*
sambal kacang	spicy peanut and chilli sauce
sambal tauco	yellow-bean relish
sambal terasi	shrimp-paste relish
sambal ulek	crushed chillis
santan	creamed coconut
sarapan	breakfast
sari buah	fruit juice
sari jeruk	orange juice
sari kaya	banana and coconut custard
sate	satay – meat kebab with peanut or soy sauce and chilli relish
sate ayam	chicken satay with peanut sauce
sate babi	pork satay
sate daging sapi	beef satay
sate kambing	mutton satay
saus selada	mayonnaise

MENU GUIDE

saus tomat	tomato ketchup
sawi	Chinese cabbage
sawo	sapodilla – brown-skinned fruit with a slight honey flavour
sayur	vegetables, vegetable dish
sayur asam	vegetable soup with tamarind
sayur kacang	red bean soup
sayur lodeh	vegetable soup with coconut milk
sayur menir	vegetable soup with minced beef
sayur oncom	*oncom* soup, clear or with coconut milk
sayur-sayuran	vegetable soup with coconut milk
segar	fresh
sekoteng	hot ginger drink, sometimes with condensed milk
selada	salad
selai	jam
seledri	type of celery
semangka	water melon
semur ayam	chicken cooked in soy sauce
semur cumi	squid cooked in soy sauce
semur daging	slices of beef cooked in soy sauce
semur daging sapi	beef cooked in soy sauce
serai	lemon grass
serundeng	fried grated coconut
setrop	fruit syrup drink
singgang ayam sumpu	chicken baked with spices and cassava leaves
singkong goreng	fried cassava (starchy vegetable)
sirsak	soursop – fruit with green, spiny skin and white, tart flesh
songklo bandang	steamed cassava flour with banana filling served in grated coconut
sop	soup
sop ayam	chicken soup
sop bakso	soup with meat or fishballs
sop bayam	spinach soup
sopi manis	liqueurs
sop kaki kambing	sheep's leg soup
sop kaki sapi	cow's leg soup
sop kapurung	Sulawesi-style vegetable and dried fish soup, thickened with sago

sop kondro	buffalo ribs soup with beans and shallots
sosis	sausage
soto ayam	chicken stew or soup
soto babat	meat stew or soup
soto daging	beef stew or soup
soto Madura	Madura-style chicken soup
soto Saudara	Sulawesi-style soup with rice noodles
sumsum	marrowbone
sumsum kukus	steamed beef marrowbone
sup	soup
susu	milk
susu segar	fresh milk
tahu	bean curd
tahu goreng	fried bean curd
tahu goreng kecap	fried bean curd with soy sauce
tahu isi	tofu stuffed with beef
tahu kupat	fried bean curd and rice cakes with coconut-milk sauce
tahu petis	fried bean curd and rice cakes with shrimp-paste and tamarind sauce
tahu sumedang	tofu with chilli sauce
tahu taoco	tofu in black bean sauce
talas	taro – vegetable similar to potato
tapai/tape	fermented sticky rice or cassava
tauge	bean sprouts
teh	tea
teh limau	lemon tea
teh manis	tea with sugar
teh susu	tea with milk
telur	egg
telur dadar	omelette
telur goreng	fried egg
telur pindang bumbu areh	spiced eggs in thick coconut sauce
telur rebus	boiled egg
tempe	cooked fermented soya beans
tepung beras	rice flour
tepung terigu	wheat flour
terasi	fermented shrimp-paste
teri	dried anchovies
terik	fried spiced beef
terung	aubergine

MENU GUIDE

terung gelatik	small white, purple, green or yellow aubergine – often eaten raw
tiram	oysters
tomat	tomatoes
tomyam	hot and sour soup with beef or fish
tongseng	goat's meat or mutton cooked in a hot coconut milk sauce
tuak	fermented palm sap drink
ubi	sweet potatoes; tapioca
ubi goreng	fried sweet potatoes
udang	prawns, shrimps
udang asam manis	sweet and sour prawns
udang bakar	charcoal-grilled marinated prawns
udang goreng	fried prawns
udang karang	lobster
udang rebus	boiled prawns
urap	vegetable salad with spicy coconut dressing
usus	intestines
usus isi telur	cow's intestines stuffed with eggs
wajik ketan	brown sticky rice cakes
wiski	whisky
wortel	carrots
zaitun	olives

SHOPS AND SERVICES

This chapter covers all sorts of shopping needs and services, and to start with you'll find some general phrases which can be used in lots of different places – many of which are named in the list below. After the general phrases come some more specific requests and sentences to use when you've found what you need, be it food, clothing, repairs, film-developing, a haircut or haggling in the market. Don't forget to refer to the mini-dictionary for items you may be looking for.

There is a great variety of shops in Indonesia, ranging from big department stores to small market stalls. Markets can open very early, while shops open at 9am. Markets also tend to close earlier than shops – some of which stay open as late as 9pm. Some shops close at midday for an hour or so on Friday (the Muslim day of prayer).

Besides shops in streets, many are sited in large covered market buildings which may be two or three storeys high. Within such an indoor market, shops selling the same kind of goods or services, such as clothes, vegetables or hairdressers, tend to be grouped in the same area.

Bargaining over the price of goods is normal practice in markets but not in department stores, large shops or supermarkets where prices are fixed. You should not expect to knock a very large percentage off the price.

Some of the most attractive souvenirs of Indonesia are clothes and household linen made of Javanese **batik**, wood carvings from Bali, embroidered **songket** cloth from West Sumatra, silver ornaments from Java, Bali and Sumatra, and jewellery, basketwork and **rattan** furniture from various regions. You can buy nearly all of them in Jakarta in the **Pasar Seni** (Art Market), in specialist shops or in boutiques in hotels.

---

ai [I], au [ow], c [ch], e [uh], e̱ [eh], i [ee], o [hot], sy [sh], u [oo], v [f]; see also pp5-6

Useful Words and Phrases

antique shop	toko barang antik
audio equipment	alat 'hi-fi'
baker's	toko roti
boutique	butik
bookshop	toko buku
buy	membeli
cake shop	toko kue
camera shop	toko kamera
carrier bag	tas
cheap	murah
china	barang pecah belah
confectioner's	toko gula-gula
craft shop	toko barang kerajinan
department store	toserba
dry cleaner's	penatu kimia
electrical goods store	toko alat-alat listrik
expensive	mahal
florist's	toko bunga
food store	toko makanan
fruit	buah
grocer's	toko makanan kelengan
hairdresser's (men's)	tukang pangkas rambut
(women's)	'salon' rias rambut
hardware shop	toko besi
indoor market	pasar tertutup
jeweller's	toko mas
ladies' wear	pakaian wanita
market	pasar
menswear	pakaian pria
optician's	toko kacamata
photography shop	toko kamera
price	harga
receipt	kwitansi
record shop	toko kaset
sale	obral

shoe repairer's	tukang sol sepatu
shoe shop	toko sepatu
shop	toko
souvenir shop	toko suvenir
sports equipment	alat-alat olahraga
sportswear	pakaian olahranga
stationer's	toko alat tulis
supermarket	toko swalayan, 'supermark<u>e</u>t'
tailor	penjahit
till	kasa
tobacconist's	toko tembakau
toyshop	toko mainan
travel agent's	biro perjalanan

Excuse me, where is/are …? *(in a department store etc)*
Maaf, di mana …?

Where is there a … shop?
Di mana toko … ?

Where is the … department?
Di mana departem<u>e</u>n … ?

Where is the main shopping area?
Di mana pusat pertokoan?

Is there an outdoor market here?
Apa ada pasar di sini?

I'd like …
Saya mau …

---

ai *[I]*, au *[ow]*, c *[ch]*, e *[uh]*, <u>e</u> *[eh]*, i *[ee]*,
o *[hot]*, sy *[sh]*, u *[oo]*, v *[f]*; *see also pp5-6*

Do you have ... ?
Apa ada ... ?

How much is this?
Berapa ini?

Where do I pay?
Di mana saya bayar?

Do you take credit cards?
Apa anda terima kartu kredit?

I think perhaps you've short-changed me
Saya pikir barangkali kembalinya kurang

Can I have a receipt?
Boleh saya minta kwitansi?

Can I have a bag, please?
Boleh saya minta kantung?

I'm just looking
Saya hanya lihat-lihat

I'll come back later
Saya akan kembali nanti

Do you have any more of these?
Apa masih ada yang seperti ini?

Have you anything cheaper?
Apa ada yang lebih murah?

Have you anything larger/smaller?
Apa ada yang lebih besar/kecil?

Can I try it (them) on?
Bol_eh saya coba?

Does it come in other colours?
Apa ada warna lain?

I'd like to exchange this, it's faulty
Saya mau tukar ini, ini rusak

I'm afraid I don't have the receipt
Maaf, saya tidak punya kwitansi

Can I have a refund?
Bol_eh saya minta kembali uang?

My camera isn't working
Kam_era saya tidak jalan

I want a 36-exposure colour film. 100 ISO
Saya mau 'film' warna isi tiga puluh enam. seratus ISO *(ee ess o)*

I'd like this film processed
Saya mau cuci 'film' ini

Matt/glossy prints
C_etak dof/mengkilap

One-hour service, please
Tolong c_etak satu jam

ai *[I]*, au *[ow]*, c *[ch]*, e *[uh]*, _e *[eh]*, i *[ee]*,
o *[hot]*, sy *[sh]*, u *[oo]*, v *[f]*; *see also pp5-6*

Where can I get this repaired?
Di mana saya bisa betulkan ini?

Can you mend this?
Apa anda dapat betulkan ini?

I'd like this skirt/these trousers dry-cleaned
Saya mau rok/celana ini dicuci-kimia

When will it/they be ready?
Kapan selesai?

I'd like to make an appointment
Saya mau buat janji

I want a cut and blow-dry
Saya mau potong dan 'blow-dry'

With conditioner
Dengan kondisioner

No conditioner, thanks
Jangan pakai kondisioner

Just a trim, please
Tolong potong sedikit saja

A bit more off here, please
Sedikit lagi di sini

Not too much off!
Jangan potong terlalu banyak!

When does the market open?
Kapan pasar buka?

Is there one today in a town nearby?
Apa ada hari ini di kota dekat sini?

What's the price per kilo?
Berapa harganya 'per kilo'?

Could you write that down?
Dapat anda tulis?

That's too much! I'll pay …
Terlalu mahal! … saja

That's fine. I'll take it
Baik. Saya ambil

I'll have a piece of that cake
Saya mau sepotong kue itu

About 250 grams
Kira-kira dua ratus lima puluh gram

About 500 grams
Kira-kira lima ratus gram

A kilo/half a kilo of oranges, please
Sekilo/setengah kilo jeruk

A quarter of a kilo of sugar, please
Seperempat kilo gula

ai [I], au [ow], c [ch], e [uh], e̱ [eh], i [ee],
o [hot], sy [sh], u [oo], v [ff]; see also pp5-6

May I taste it?
Boleh saya coba?

No, I don't like it
Tidak, saya tidak suka

That's very nice. I'll take ten
Enak sekali. Saya ambil sepuluh

It isn't what I wanted
Itu bukan yang saya inginkan

THINGS YOU'LL SEE

agen perjalanan	travel agent's
alat tulis	stationery
bagian	department
bagian wanita	ladies' department
bayar di sini	please pay here
buka	open
bunga	flowers
dikurangi	reduced
harga	price
harga pasti	fixed price
jual murah	special offer
kamar pas	fitting room
kasa/kassa	till
kasir	till
keperluan kantor	office supplies
kios	newspaper kiosk
lantai atas	upper floor
lantai bawah	lower floor
maaf, jangan sentuh	please do not touch
mainan	toys
obral	sale

→

pakaian pria	menswear
pakaian wanita	ladies' clothing
pangkas rambut	barber's
pasar	market
Pasar Seni	Art Market
penatu kimia	dry cleaner's
proses film	film processing
repararsi sepatu	shoe repairs
salon rias rambut	ladies' hairdresser's
sayuran	vegetables
swalayan	self-service
toko alat tulis	stationer's
toko barang kerajinan	craft shop
toko buku	bookshop
toko bunga	flower shop, florist
toko eskrim	ice cream shop
toko kaset	record shop
toko kelontong	grocer
toko keperluan sekolah	school supplies shop
toko kue	cake shop
toko pecah-belah	china shop
toko roti	bread shop, bakery
toko sepatu	shoe shop
toko tembakau	tobacconist's
toserba	department store
tutup	closed
uang ganti tidak diberikan	we cannot give cash refunds

THINGS YOU'LL HEAR

Apa anda sudah dilayani?
Are you being served?

→

ai *[I]*, au *[ow]*, c *[ch]*, e *[uh]*, e̲ *[eh]*, i *[ee]*,
o *[hot]*, sy *[sh]*, u *[oo]*, v *[f]*; *see also pp5-6*

Apa anda ada uang yang lebih kecil?
Have you anything smaller? (*money*)

Maaf, persediaan kami sudah habis
I'm sorry, we're out of stock

Hanya ini yang tersedia
This is all we have

Ada yang lainnya?
Will there be anything else?

Anda perlu berapa banyak?
How much would you like?

Mau potong model apa?
How would you like it cut?

BARS AND ENTERTAINMENT

Depending on the size of the town or city, there are various kinds of entertainment to be had. Even the smallest town will have a cinema and restaurants. However, bars, nightclubs, discos, karaoke bars (very popular with Indonesians), theatres and rock concerts are more often found in large towns and cities. Most medium-to-large hotels provide the sort of entertainment it is assumed Westerners like, such as discos and bars.

Apart from beer, most ordinary cafés and bars do not serve alcohol. Only the more expensive bars serve alcoholic drinks. Most Indonesian towns have a Chinese quarter, and it is in these areas that it is easiest to buy alcohol and find bars in a relatively small town. You may either order your drink at the bar yourself or sit elsewhere and be waited on. Tea and coffee are usually available in all kinds of establishments.

In some parts of Indonesia, you will find performances of traditional theatre, dance, **wayang kulit** (shadow-play) etc. Traditionally, performances of **wayang kulit** begin some time after sunset, after evening prayers, and continue all night until sunrise, just before dawn prayers. If you attend such a performance, don't be surprised if most of the audience are apparently taking no notice whatsoever of the performance, either sitting around talking, drinking coffee or falling asleep! The stories are usually well-known and the social aspect of the occasion is considered to be more important than the details of the performance itself. If you don't think you can face such an all-night marathon, don't worry! Shortened versions of local traditional theatrical and dance forms are performed in most towns. The larger hotels put on a variety of modern floor shows or displays of traditional dancing.

For contemporary arts and culture, you could visit **Taman Ismail Marzuki** (TIM) on Jalan Cikini Raya in Jakarta which presents both traditional and contemporary Indonesian arts and

ai *[I]*, au *[ow]*, c *[ch]*, e *[uh]*, ę *[eh]*, i *[ee]*,
o *[hot]*, sy *[sh]*, u *[oo]*, v *[f]*; *see also pp5-6*

culture, as well as overseas performers. Most large towns provide an outlet for contemporary as well as traditional art forms.

Depending on the region, you may come across local traditional festivals and ceremonies. For example, in Bali, temple festivals abound with colourful processions. In Yogyakarta you might be lucky enough to witness the **Garebeg**, an Islamic festival which includes a procession of all the **karaton** (palace) guards in their variety of uniforms carrying huge mounds of rice to the mosque for blessing, and later for distribution to the people present. This particular festival takes place three times a year. Check with the local tourist office for details of any such festivals, as very few fall on the same date each year.

An enjoyable evening can be spent in the **pasar malam** (night market). All Indonesian towns hold a night market, usually selling an incredible variety of food and, after having enjoyed a pleasant stroll around the stalls, you can sit down at one of the **warung** (outdoor restaurants) and sample some of the local fare.

USEFUL WORDS AND PHRASES

bar	bar *(bar-r)*
bar girl	pelayan bar *(bar-r)*
barman	pelayan bar *(bar-r)*
box office	loket
cabaret	kabaret
café	kafe
cinema	bioskop
coca cola®	'coca cola'®
cocktail bar	'cocktail' bar *(bar-r)*
concert	konser
disco	disko
drink *(noun)*	minuman
film	'film'
folk dancing	tari rakyat
gin and tonic	jin dan tonik
group *(rock etc)*	grup
lemonade	limun

nightclub	kelab malam, 'nightclub'
night market	pasar malam
opera	'opera'
orange juice	sari jeruk
orchestra	orkes
play *(noun)*	sandiwara
puppet show	pertunjukan wayang golek
red wine	anggur merah
seat	tempat duduk
shadow-play	wayang kulit
theatre	teater
ticket	karcis
vodka	'vodka'
white wine	anggur putih
whisky	wiski

What would you like (to drink)?
Anda mau minum apa?

A beer, please *(answer to the above question)*
Saya mau bir

(independent request)
Minta bir satu

Nothing for me, thanks
Tidak, terima kasih

I'll get this one
Ini giliran saya

I'd like …
Saya mau …

---

ai *[I]*, au *[ow]*, c *[ch]*, e *[uh]*, e̲ *[eh]*, i *[ee]*,
o *[hot]*, sy *[sh]*, u *[oo]*, v *[f]*; see also pp5-6

Cheers!
Selamat!

The same again, please
Seperti yang tadi

Would you like another drink?
Apa anda mau minuman lagi?

I don't drink/smoke
Saya tidak minum/merokok

Do you mind if I smoke?
Anda tidak berkeberatan kalau saya merokok?

What's on tonight?
Ada tontonan apa malam ini?

I would like to …
Saya mau …

Let's go to …
Mari kita pergi ke …

Is there a concert on tonight?
Apa ada konser malam ini?

What time does it start?
Jam berapa mulainya?

Where can we see Indonesian traditional dancing?
Di mana kita dapat menonton tari tradisional Indonesia?

I'd like three tickets for tomorrow
Saya mau tiga karcis untuk besok

Is there a good nightclub near here?
Apa ada kelab malam yang bagus dekat sini?

Would you like to dance?
Anda mau dansa?

No, thank you. I'm with a friend
Tidak, terima kasih. Saya bersama teman

THINGS YOU'LL SEE

akan datang	coming soon
bioskop	cinema
dangdut	Hindi-influenced dance and music
dangdut bar	bar where *dangdut* is danced to
daftar harga	price list
film baru	new film
kelab malam	nightclub
malam ini	tonight
pameran lukisan/seni	art exhibition
pertunjukan	show
pertunjukan adat	traditional performance
pertunjukan musik	musical performance
semua umur	all ages
17 tahun ke atas	over 16s only
wayang golek	wooden puppets
wayang kulit	shadow-play
wayang wong	traditional drama (with actors)

---

ai *[I]*, au *[ow]*, c *[ch]*, e *[uh]*, e̱ *[eh]*, i *[ee]*,
o *[hot]*, sy *[sh]*, u *[oo]*, v *[f]*; *see also pp5-6*

SPORT

The intense heat and humid conditions are not very conducive to the more strenuous outdoor sporting activities and most Indonesians are as yet not very interested in sport for leisure. That said, sport is becoming more popular in Indonesia, and the government is encouraging an increased emphasis on sport and physical education in schools and colleges.

Until recently, Indonesia dominated the world badminton championships, and it is still considered to be the national sport. Tennis is proving increasingly popular, as are football and basketball. Certainly, most young men in Indonesia are familiar with the European football league and most large towns have a football team and a football stadium. The local tourist office is the best place to enquire about local sporting facilities. Traditionally, the Malay martial art form **pencak silat** was taught to boys at the local mosque schools, and is taught today to boys and girls alike. Most Indonesians, however, are happiest sitting with friends in a coffee shop, playing games like chess, dominoes and backgammon. A game of chess provides an excellent means by which to overcome the language barrier, but beware, the standard of play is very high!

The seas around the archipelago can prove very dangerous indeed, which might serve to explain why the Indonesians are not a nation of swimmers. Do not be surprised if most people you meet can't swim. Even the experienced swimmer should avoid beaches that are generally not accepted as safe because of the dangers of undertow, cross-currents and tides. In some areas, there are also hazards from sharks, jellyfish and water snakes. If in doubt, stick to hotel pools and supervised beach areas. Most hotels allow non-residents to use their pool for a small fee which usually includes use of towels, lockers and deckchairs. A small number of the larger hotels have gymnasiums which are also open to non-residents.

Surfboards, sailboards, deckchairs and beach umbrellas can be hired on popular beaches. On some beaches, itinerant masseuses offer their services and there are people selling food, drink and souvenirs. A nearby hotel pool can serve as a welcome break from such constant attention! Although Indonesians themselves, especially the women, rarely go into the water, they nevertheless enjoy going down to the beach on a Sunday, usually their only day off. On some beaches, mainly in Bali, windsurfing and water-skiing are available.

There are also opportunities to go skin-diving but you must always be accompanied by a licensed guide. Coral collecting and harpooning are illegal.

USEFUL WORDS AND PHRASES

athletics	atletik
badminton	bulu tangkis
ball	bola
beach	pantai
bicycle	sepeda
canoe	kano
canoeing	berkano
current	arus
deckchair	kursi dek
dive (verb)	melompat
diving board	papan lompat
diving mask	masker selam
fishing	mengail
fishing rod	joran
flippers	fliper
football	sepakbola
football match	pertandingan sepakbola
goggles	kacamata selam
golf	golf
golf course	lapangan golf
gymnastics	jimnasik
jogging	joging

ai *[I]*, au *[ow]*, c *[ch]*, e *[uh]*, e *[eh]*, i *[ee]*, o *[hot]*, sy *[sh]*, u *[oo]*, v *[f]*; *see also pp5-6*

lake	danau
mast	tiang
mountaineering	naik gunung
oars	dayung, kayuh
oxygen bottles	botol oksigen
pedal boat	perahu 'pedal'
racket	raket
riding	naik kuda
rowing boat	perahu dayung
run (verb)	lari
sailboard	selancar angin
sailing	berlayar
scuba	'scuba'
scuba diving	'scuba diving'
sea	laut
skin diving	olahraga selam
snorkel	'snorkel'
stadium	stadion
sunshade	payung
swim (verb)	berenang
swimming pool	kolam renang
tennis	tenis
tennis court	lapangan tenis
tennis racket	raket tenis
underwater fishing	menangkap ikan bawah air
volleyball	bola voli
walking	berjalan
water-skiing	ber-ski air
water-skis	ski air
wave	ombak
wet suit	pakaian selam
windsurfing	selancar angin
yacht	kapal pesiar

How do I get to the beach?
Bagaimana saya pergi ke pantai?

Let's go swimming
Mari kita berenang

How deep is the water here?
Berapa dalam air di sini?

Is there an indoor/outdoor pool here?
Apa ada kolam tertutup/terbuka di sini?

Is it safe to swim here?
Apa aman berenang di sini?

I'd like to go scuba diving
Saya ingin 'scuba diving'

Can I fish here?
Boleh saya menangkap ikan di sini?

I would like to hire a sunshade
Saya mau sewa payung

How much does it cost per hour/day?
Berapa bayarannya per jam/hari?

I would like to take water-skiing lessons
Saya mau ambil les ski air

There's something wrong with these water-skis
Ski air ini rusak

Where can I hire ...?
Di mana saya dapat menyewa ...?

---

ai *[I]*, au *[ow]*, c *[ch]*, e *[uh]*, e *[eh]*, i *[ee]*,
o *[hot]*, sy *[sh]*, u *[oo]*, v *[f]*; *see also pp5-6*

THINGS YOU'LL SEE

awas!	danger!
bahaya!	danger!
bukan pantai umum	private beach
daerah terlarang	restricted area
dilarang berenang	no swimming
dilarang kamping	no camping
dilarang menangkap ikan	no fishing
dilarang menyelam	no diving
fasilitas olahraga	sporting facilities
kapal layar	sailing boats
karcis	tickets
kursi dek	deckchairs
lapangan pacuan kuda	race course
lapangan sepakbola	football pitch
lapangan tenis	tennis court
les ski air	water-skiing lessons
olahraga air	water sports
pantai	beach
pantai umum	public beach
pelabuhan	port
perahu untuk disewakan	boats for hire
pertolongan pertama	first aid
polisi pelabuhan	harbour police
pusat olahraga	sports centre
sepeda	bicycles
stadion	stadium
sumber air panas	hot springs
tikar untuk disewakan	mats for hire
untuk disewakan	for hire

POST OFFICES AND BANKS

Local post offices are open from 8am to 1pm from Monday to Thursday, but main post offices stay open until 5pm. All post offices shut at 11am on Fridays (the Muslim day of prayer) and at 1pm on Saturdays. They do not open on Sundays.

Post boxes are red and square. Stamps can also be bought in some shops at a slightly higher price than at the post office. Banks are open from 8am to 12.30pm and 1.30 to 4pm from Monday to Friday and from 8am to 12.30pm on Saturdays. Foreign currency can also be exchanged in the larger hotels, but at less advantageous rates.

The Indonesian unit of currency is the **rupiah**. The smallest coin in circulation is 5 **rupiah** and the largest denomination is Rp500. The smallest note is Rp100 and the largest Rp50,000.

Credit cards are accepted in large shops and hotels.

USEFUL WORDS AND PHRASES

airmail	pos udara
bank	bank (bunk)
change (verb)	menukar
cheque	cek
collection	pengambilan
credit card	kartu kredit
customs form	formulir bea-cukai
delivery	pengiriman
exchange rate	kurs
fax	'fax'
form	formulir
international money order	poswesel internasional
letter	surat
mail (noun)	surat
package/parcel	paket

---

ai *[I]*, au *[ow]*, c *[ch]*, e *[uh]*, e *[eh]*, i *[ee]*,
o *[hot]*, sy *[sh]*, u *[oo]*, v *[f]*; *see also pp5-6*

post	pos
postage	porto
post box	kotak surat
postcard	kartu pos
postman	tukang pos
post office	kantor pos
pound sterling	pon sterling (*stair-ling*)
registered letter	surat terdaftar
stamp	perangko
surface mail	surat biasa, pos biasa
telegram	telegram
traveller's cheque	cek perjalanan

How much is a letter/postcard to England?
Berapa surat/kartu pos ke Inggris?

I would like three 100 rupiah stamps
Saya mau tiga perangko seratus rupiah

I want to have this letter sent registered post
Saya mau surat ini dikirim tercatat

I want to send this parcel to England
Saya mau mengirim paket ini ke Inggris

How long does the post to America take?
Berapa lama surat ke Amerika?

Is there any mail for me?
Apa ada surat untuk saya?

I'd like to send a telegram/fax
Saya mau mengirim telegram/'fax' ke

This is to go airmail
Ini dikirim lewat udara

I'd like to change this into rupiah
Saya mau menukar ini ke rupiah

I'd like that in 1,000 rupiah notes
Tolong berikan dalam lembaran seribu rupiah

Can I cash these traveller's cheques?
Apa saya bisa menguangkan cek perjalanan ini?

THINGS YOU'LL SEE

alamat	address
barang cetakan	printed matter
biaya	charges
jam buka	opening hours
kantor pos	post office
kasa/kasir	cashier
kotak surat	letterbox
kurs uang	exchange rate
luar negeri	abroad
mengisi	fill in
ongkos	fee
pengambilan	withdrawals
pengirim	sender
penyetoran	deposits
perangko	stamp
porto luar negeri	overseas postage
pos dalam negeri	inland mail
pos udara	airmail
si alamat	addressee
surat	letter
tempat tukar uang	exchange
valuta asing	foreign currency

---

ai [I], au [ow], c [ch], e [uh], e [eh], i [ee],
o [hot], sy [sh], u [oo], v [f]; see also pp5-6

TELEPHONES

There are public phones in **Kantor Telepon** (Telephone Offices),
wartel (telephone shops), large stores and at the roadside.
Calls within Indonesia and abroad can be dialled direct, but
in hotels, Telephone Offices and phone shops you can ask the
operator to dial for you. Coin-operated phones can only be
used for local calls, but those taking phonecards (sold in
Telephone Offices and telephone shops) can also be used for
long-distance and international calls.

The dialling tone is a continuous buzz, the ringing tone a
repeated single bleep, and the engaged tone is a rapid
succession of pips.

USEFUL WORDS AND PHRASES

call *(noun)*	panggilan telepon
(verb)	menelepon
cardphone	telepon umum kartu
code	kode
crossed line	silang hubungan
dial *(verb)*	memutar
dialling tone	nada putar
emergency	darurat
enquiries	penerangan
extension	pesawat
international call	panggilan internasional
number	nomor
operator	'operator'
pay-phone	telepon umum
phonecard	kartu telepon
receiver	gagang telepon
reverse charge call	'collect call'
telephone	telepon
telephone box	telepon umum
telephone directory	buku telepon
wrong number	salah sambung

Where is the nearest phone box?
Di mana telepon umum yang paling dekat?

Is there a telephone directory?
Apa ada buku telepon?

I would like the directory for Jakarta
Saya mau buku telepon untuk Jakarta

Can I call abroad from here?
Apa saya boleh menelepon ke luar negeri dari sini?

How much is a call to Bandung?
Berapa satu panggilan telepon ke Bandung?

I would like to reverse the charges
Saya mau 'collect call'

I would like a number in Jakarta
Saya mau nomor telepon di Jakarta

Hello, this is Anne speaking
Halo, ini Anne bicara

Is that Oking?
Apa ini Oking?

Speaking
Saya sendiri

I would like to speak to Reno
Saya mau bicara dengan Reno

---

ai *[I]*, au *[ow]*, c *[ch]*, e *[uh]*, e *[eh]*, i *[ee]*,
o *[hot]*, sy *[sh]*, u *[oo]*, v *[f]*; *see also pp5-6*

Extension 21955, please
Pesawat dua satu sembilan lima lima

Please tell him/her David called
Tolong beri tahu dia David menelepon

Ask him/her to call me back, please
Tolong minta dia supaya menelepon saya

My number is 28663
Nomor saya dua delapan enam enam tiga

Do you know where he/she is?
Apa anda tahu di mana dia?

When will he/she be back?
Kapan dia akan kembali?

Could you leave him/her a message?
Apa anda mau tinggalkan pesan untuknya?

I'll ring back later
Saya akan bel lagi dia nanti

Sorry, wrong number
Maaf, salah sambung

THINGS YOU'LL SEE

biaya	charges
darurat	emergency
halaman kuning	yellow pages
Kantor Telepon	Telephone Office
kartu telepon	phonecard
panggilan interlokal	long-distance call
panggilan internasional	international call
panggilan lokal	local call
penerangan	enquiries
rusak	out of order, faults service
SLI	international direct dialling
SLJJ	STD
telepon umum	public telephone
telepon umum kartu	cardphone
wartel	telephone shop

REPLIES YOU MAY BE GIVEN

Anda mau bicara dengan siapa?
Who would you like to speak to?

Anda salah sambung
You've got the wrong number

Siapa bicara?
Who's speaking?

Telepon anda nomor berapa?
What is your number?

Maaf, dia sedang keluar
Sorry, he/she's not in

→

ai *[I]*, au *[ow]*, c *[ch]*, e *[uh]*, e *[eh]*, i *[ee]*,
o *[hot]*, sy *[sh]*, u *[oo]*, v *[f]*; *see also pp5-6*

Dia akan kembali jam enam
He/she will be back at six o'clock

Apa anda bisa telepon lagi besok?
Could you call again tomorrow?

Saya akan beri tahu dia anda menelepon
I'll tell him/her you called

EMERGENCIES

Information on local health services can be obtained from your hotel or local tourist information office. Emergency telephone numbers are as follows: ambulance – 118; police – 110; fire brigade – 113.

USEFUL WORDS AND PHRASES

accident	kecelakaan
ambulance	ambulans
assault *(verb)*	menyerang
break down	mogok
burglary	pencurian
casualty department	bagian gawat darurat
crash *(noun)*	tabrakan
fire	kebakaran
fire brigade	pasukan pemadam kebakaran
flood *(noun)*	banjir
garage *(for repairs)*	bengkel
lose	hilang
pickpocket	copet
police	polisi
police station	kantor polisi
rob	merampok
steal	mencuri
theft	pencurian
tow *(verb)*	menarik

Help!
Tolong!

Look out!
Awas!

ai *[I]*, au *[ow]*, c *[ch]*, e *[uh]*, e̱ *[eh]*, i *[ee]*,
o *[hot]*, sy *[sh]*, u *[oo]*, v *[f]*; *see also pp5-6*

This is an emergency!
Ini keadaan darurat!

Please send an ambulance to …
Tolong kirim ambulans ke …

Please come to …
Tolong datang ke …

My address is …
Alamat saya …

We've had a break-in
Rumah kami didobrak pencuri

There's a fire at …
Ada kebakaran di …

Someone's been injured/knocked down
Ada orang cedera/ditabrak

My passport/car has been stolen
Paspor/mobil saya dicuri

I've lost my traveller's cheques
Cek perjalanan saya hilang

I want to report a stolen credit card
Saya mau melaporkan kartu kredit saya dicuri

It was stolen from my room
Dicuri dari kamar saya

I lost it on the train
Hilang di kereta api

My luggage has gone missing
Kopor saya hilang

Has my luggage turned up yet?
Apa kopor saya sudah muncul?

My car's been hit
Mobil saya ditabrak

My car's been broken into
Mobil saya didobrak orang

The registration number is …
Nomor pelatnya …

I've been mugged
Saya ditodong

My son's missing
Anak laki-laki saya hilang

I've locked myself out
Saya terkunci di luar

He/she's drowning
Dia tenggelam

He/she can't swim
Dia tidak bisa berenang

---

ai *[I]*, au *[ow]*, c *[ch]*, e *[uh]*, e *[eh]*, i *[ee]*,
o *[hot]*, sy *[sh]*, u *[oo]*, v *[f]*; *see also pp5-6*

THINGS YOU'LL SEE

bagian gawat darurat	casualty department
darurat	emergencies
kantor polisi	police station
kebakaran	fire
pelayanan 24 jam	24-hour service
polisi	police
polisi lalu-lintas	traffic police
polisi pelabuhan	harbour police
PPPK	first aid
putar ...	dial ...
RSU	hospital
rumah sakit	hospital

THINGS YOU'LL HEAR

Apa alamat anda?
What's your address?

Di mana anda?
Where are you?

Apa anda bisa melukiskannya?
Can you describe it/him?

HEALTH

Make sure you get all the necessary injections (typhoid, hepatitis, cholera etc) and malaria pills before you leave for Indonesia. Start taking the malaria pills before you go.

Medical care can be expensive, so you are strongly advised to take out medical insurance when making your travel arrangements. If you become seriously ill, ask the advice of the Embassy as to which doctors they recommend.

Common medicines like aspirin and cough pastilles can be bought in a **toko obat** (medicine shop), but a doctor's prescription can only be dealt with at an **apotek** (pharmacy) or a medicine shop showing the sign **terima resep dokter** (doctors' prescriptions accepted).

USEFUL WORDS AND PHRASES

accident	kecelakaan
ambulance	ambulans
anaemic	anemik
appendicitis	radang usus buntu
appendix	usus buntu
aspirin	aspirin (*ass-pee-rin*)
asthma	asma
backache	sakit pinggang
bandage	pembalut
bite (*noun*)	gigitan
bladder	kandung kencing
blister	lepuh
blood	darah
blood donor	donor darah
burn (*noun*)	luka bakar
cancer	kangker
chemist's	apotek
chest	dada

---

ai *[I]*, au *[ow]*, c *[ch]*, e *[uh]*, e *[eh]*, i *[ee]*, o *[hot]*, sy *[sh]*, u *[oo]*, v *[f]*; *see also pp5-6*

chickenpox	cacar air
cold *(noun)*	pilek, selesma
concussion	gegar
constipation	sembelit
contact lenses	kontak lens
corn	katimumul
cough *(noun, verb)*	batuk
cut	luka
dentist	dokter gigi
diabetes	diabetes *(dee-abehtehss)*
diarrhoea	diare
dizzy	pusing
doctor	dokter
earache	sakit telinga
fever	demam
filling	tambal gigi
first aid	pertolongan pertama
flu	'flu'
fracture	retak
German measles	biring peluh
glasses	kacamata
haemorrhage	pendarahan
headache	sakit kepala
heart	jantung
heart attack	serangan jantung
hospital	rumahsakit
ill	sakit
indigestion	salah cerna
injection	suntik
itch	gatal
kidney	ginjal
lump	benjol
malaria	malaria *(malahree-a)*
malaria pills	obat malaria *(malahree-a)*
measles	campak
migraine	sakit kepala migren
mumps	gondong

nausea	mual
nurse	perawat
operation	operasi
optician	ahli kacamata
pain	sakit
penicillin	penisilin
plaster *(sticky)*	plester
plaster of Paris	gips
pneumonia	radang paru-paru
pregnant	hamil
prescription	resep
rheumatism	rematik
scald *(noun)*	luka kena air panas
scratch *(noun)*	lecet
smallpox	cacar
sore throat	sakit tenggorokan
splinter	suban kayu
sprain *(noun)*	keseleo
sting *(noun)*	sengatan
stomach	perut
temperature	suhu
tonsils	amandel
toothache	sakit gigi
travel sickness	mabuk perjalanan
typhoid	penyakit tipus
ulcer	borok
vaccination	vaksinasi
vomit *(verb)*	muntah
whooping cough	batuk rejan

I have a pain in …
… saya sakit

---

ai *[I]*, au *[ow]*, c *[ch]*, e *[uh]*, e̲ *[eh]*, i *[ee]*,
o *[hot]*, sy *[sh]*, u *[oo]*, v *[f]*; *see also pp5-6*

I do not feel well
Saya tidak enak badan

I feel faint
Saya merasa pusing

I feel sick
Saya merasa mual

I feel dizzy
Saya merasa pusing

It hurts here
Sakit di sini

It's a sharp pain
Sakit menusuk

It's a dull pain
Tidak begitu sakit

It hurts all the time
Terus sakit

It only hurts now and then
Hanya sakit kadang-kadang

It hurts when you touch it
Sakit kalau disentuh

It hurts more at night
Lebih sakit di malam hari

It stings
Pedih

It aches
Sakit

I have a temperature
Saya demam

I need a prescription for …
Saya perlu resep untuk …

I normally take …
Biasanya saya minum …

I'm allergic to …
Saya alergi terhadap …

Have you got anything for …?
Apa anda punya obat untuk …?

Do I need a prescription for …?
Apa saya perlu resep untuk …?

I have lost a filling
Tambal gigi saya copot

---

ai *[I]*, au *[ow]*, c *[ch]*, e *[uh]*, e *[eh]*, i *[ee]*,
o *[hot]*, sy *[sh]*, u *[oo]*, v *[f]*; *see also pp5-6*

THINGS YOU'LL SEE

ahli kacamata	optician
apotek	chemist
bagian gawat darurat	emergency department
bidan	midwife
buka sampai jam ...	open until ...
dokter	doctor
dokter bedah	surgeon
dokter gigi	dentist
dokter umum	general practitioner
kamar periksa	consulting room
kamar tunggu	waiting room
klinik bersalin	maternity clinic
obat	medicine
PPPK	first aid
puskesmas	community health centre
resep	prescription
rumah sakit	hospital
rumah sakit bersalin	maternity hospital
sinar X	X-ray
spesialis telinga, hidung dan tenggorokan	ear, nose and throat specialist
terima resep dokter	doctors' prescriptions accepted
toko obat	medicine shop

THINGS YOU'LL HEAR

Tiap kalinya minum ... pel/tablet
Take ... pills/tablets at a time

Dengan air
With water

Kunyah
Chew them

Satu/dua/tiga kali sehari
Once/twice/three times a day

Hanya kalau anda pergi tidur
Only when you go to bed

Apa yang biasa anda minum?
What do you normally take?

Saya pikir anda harus pergi ke dokter
I think you should see a doctor

Maaf kami tidak punya itu
I'm sorry, we don't have that

Untuk itu anda perlu resep
For that you need a prescription

---

ai *[I]*, au *[ow]*, c *[ch]*, e *[uh]*, e̱ *[eh]*, i *[ee]*,
o *[hot]*, sy *[sh]*, u *[oo]*, v *[f]*; *see also pp5-6*

CONVERSION TABLES

DISTANCES

A mile is 1.6km. To convert kilometres to miles, divide the km by 8 and multiply by 5. Convert miles to km by dividing the miles by 5 and multiplying by 8.

miles	0.62	1.24	1.86	2.43	3.11	3.73	4.35	6.21
miles *or* km	1	2	3	4	5	6	7	10
km	1.61	3.22	4.83	6.44	8.05	9.66	11.27	16.10

WEIGHTS

The kilogram is equivalent to 2lb 3oz. To convert kg to lbs, divide by 5 and multiply by 11. One ounce is about 28 grams, and eight ounces about 227 grams; 1lb is therefore about 454 grams.

lbs	2.20	4.41	6.61	8.82	11.02	13.23	19.84	22.04
lbs *or* kg	1	2	3	4	5	6	9	10
kg	0.45	0.91	1.36	1.81	2.27	2.72	4.08	4.53

TEMPERATURE

To convert Celsius degrees into Fahrenheit, the accurate method is to multiply the °C figure by 1.8 and add 32. Similarly, to convert °F to °C, subtract 32 from the °F figure and divide by 1.8.

| °C | -10 | 0 | 5 | 10 | 20 | 30 | 36.9 | 40 | 100 |
| °F | 14 | 32 | 41 | 50 | 68 | 86 | 98.4 | 104 | 212 |

LIQUIDS

A litre is about 1.75 pints; a gallon is roughly 4.5 litres.

gals	0.22	0.44	1.10	2.20	4.40	6.60	11.00
gals *or* litres	1	2	5	10	20	30	50
litres	4.54	9.10	22.73	45.46	90.92	136.40	227.30

TYRE PRESSURES

| lb/sq in | 18 | 20 | 22 | 24 | 26 | 28 | 30 | 33 |
| kg/sq cm | 1.3 | 1.4 | 1.5 | 1.7 | 1.8 | 2.0 | 2.1 | 2.3 |

MINI-DICTIONARY

about: about 16 kira-kira enam belas
accelerator pedal gas
accident kecelakaan
accommodation akomodasi
ache: it aches sakit
adaptor (*electrical*) adaptor
address alamat
adhesive perekat
after setelah
aftershave aftershave
again lagi
against kontra
Aids aids
air (*noun*) udara
air-conditioning AC
aircraft pesawat terbang
air freshener pewangi ruangan, Glade®
air hostess pramugari
airline perusahaan penerbangan
airport (*small*) lapangan terbang
    (*large*) bandar udara
aisle gang
alarm clock beker
alcohol alkohol
all semua
    all the streets semua jalan
    that's all, thanks cukup sekian, terima
    kasih
almost hampir
alone sendiri
already sudah
always selalu
am: I am *see p6*
ambulance ambulans
America Amerika
American (*man*) pria Amerika
    (*woman*) wanita Amerika
    (*adj*) ... Amerika
and dan

ankle pergelangan kaki
another (*different*) ... yang lain
    (*one more*) ... satu lagi
    another room kamar yang lain
    another coffee, please kopi satu lagi
antique shop toko barang antik
antiseptic antiseptik
apartment apartmen
aperitif minuman sebelum makan
appetite nafsu makan
apple apel
application form formulir permohonan
appointment janji
apricot aprikot
are *see p6*
arm lengan
art seni
art gallery galeri seni
artist seniman
as: as soon as possible selekas
    mungkin
ashtray asbak
asleep: he/she's asleep dia tidur
aspirin aspirin
at: at the post office di kantor pos
    at night di malam hari
    at 2 o'clock pada jam dua
attractive menarik
aunt bibi
Australia Australia
Australian (*man*) pria Australia
    (*woman*) wanita Australia
    (*adj*) ... Australia
automatic otomatis
away: is it far away? apa itu jauh?
    go away! pergi!
awful mengerikan
axe kapak
axle as

baby bayi
back *(not front)* belakang
  (body) punggung
  to come back kembali
bacon spek
bad buruk
bag *(handbag)* tas
  (plastic) kantung
baggage claim pengambilan barang
bait umpan
bake membakar
baker's toko roti
balcony balkon
Bali Bali
Balinese *(noun)* orang Bali
  (adj) ... Bali
ball bola
ballpoint pen bolpoin
bamboo bambu
banana pisang
band *(musicians)* grup musik
bandage pembalut
bank bank
banknote uang kertas
bar *(drinks)* bar
  bar of chocolate sepotong coklat
barbecue tempat pembakaran sate
barber's tempat pemangkas rambut
bargain harga murah
basement lantai bawah tanah
basin *(sink)* wastafel
basket keranjang
bath mandi
  (tub) bak mandi
  to have a bath mandi
bathroom kamar mandi
battery batere
bazaar pasar
beach pantai
beans buncis
beard jenggot
beautiful cantik
because karena
bed tempat tidur

bed linen seprai
bedroom kamar tidur
beef daging sapi
beer bir
before sebelum
beginner pemula
behind di belakang
beige coklat muda
bell *(church)* lonceng
  (door) bel
below di bawah
belt ikat pinggang
beside di samping
best terbaik
better lebih baik
between ... antara ...
bicycle sepeda
big besar
bikini bikini
bill rekening
bin liner kantung plastik besar
bird burung
birthday ulang tahun
  happy birthday! selamat hari ulang
  tahun!
birthday present hadiah ulang
  tahun
biscuit biskuit
bite *(noun)* gigitan
  (verb) menggigit
bitter pahit
black hitam
blanket selimut
blind *(cannot see)* buta
blinds tirai
blister lepuh
blond(e) blon
blood darah
blouse blus
blue biru
boarding card kartu naik pesawat
boat kapal
  (smaller) perahu
body badan

boil (verb: of water etc) mendidih
(potatoes etc) merebus
bolt (noun: on door) gerendel
(verb) menggerendel
bone tulang
bonnet (car) kap mesin
book (noun) buku
(verb) memesan
bookshop toko buku
boot (car) tempat bagasi
(footwear) sepatu lars
border perbatasan
boring membosankan
born: I was born in … saya lahir di …
both keduanya
both of them keduanya
both of us kami berdua
both … and … baik … maupun …
bottle botol
bottle-opener pembuka botol
bottom dasar
(part of body) pantat
bowl mangkok
box kotak
box office loket
boy anak laki-laki
boyfriend pacar
bra beha
bracelet gelang
braces bretel
brake (noun) rem
(verb) merem
brandy brandi
bread roti
breakdown (nervous) dipresi
I've had a breakdown (car) mobil
saya mogok
break down (car) mogok
breakfast sarapan
breathe bernafas
I can't breathe saya tidak dapat
bernafas
bridge jembatan
(game) bridge

briefcase tas
British Inggris
brochure brosur
broken patah
broken leg kaki patah
brooch bros
brother saudara laki-laki
brown coklat
bruise lecet
brush (noun: hair) sikat
(paint) kwas
(for sweeping) sapu
(verb: hair) menyikat
(floor) menyapu
bucket ember
Buddha Budha
Buddhism Budhisme
Buddhist (noun) orang Budha
building bangunan
bumper bemper
burglar maling
burn (noun) luka bakar
(verb) membakar
bus bis
business bisnis
it's none of your business bukan
urusan anda
bus station setasiun bis
busy (occupied) sibuk
(bar etc) penuh
but tetapi
butcher's toko daging
butter mentega
button kancing
buy membeli
by: by the window dekat jendela
by Friday sebelum Jumat
by myself saya sendiri

cabbage kol
café cafe, rumah makan
cake kue kik
cake shop toko kue
calculator kalkulator

call: what's it called? apa namanya?
camcorder kamkorder
camera kamera
campsite tempat kamping
camshaft poros silinder mesin
can (tin) kaleng
can: can I have ...? boleh saya minta ...?
Canada Kanada
Canadian (man) pria Kanada
  (woman) wanita Kanada
  (adj) ... Kanada
cancer kangker
candle lilin
canoe kano
cap (bottle) tutup
  (hat) topi
car mobil
caravan karavan
carburettor karburetor
card kartu
cardigan baju sweter
careful hati-hati
  be careful! hati-hati!
carpet karpet
carriage (train) gerbong
carrot wortel
case (suitcase) kopor
cash (verb) menguangkan
  to pay cash bayar kontan
cash dispenser a.t.m.
cassette kaset
cassette player kaset dek
cat kucing
cauliflower blumkol
cave gua
Celebes Sulawesi
cemetery kuburan
centre pusat
certificate sertifikat
chair kursi
change (noun: money) uang kecil
  (money back) uang kembali
  (verb: money) menukar
  (clothes) ganti

cheap murah
cheers! (toast) selamat!
cheese keju
chemist's apotik
cheque cek
cheque book buku cek
cheque card kartu cek
cherry ceri
chess catur
chest (part of body) dada
  (furniture) peti
chewing gum permen karet
chicken ayam
  (meat) daging ayam
child anak
children anak-anak
china barang-barang dari
  porselen
China Cina
Chinese (man) pria Cina
  (woman) wanita Cina
  (adj) ... Cina
chips cip
chocolate coklat
  box of chocolates satu dus
  coklat
chop (food) sepotong daging
  (verb: to cut) memotong
Christian Kristen
Christian name nama depan
church gereja
cigar cerutu
cigarette rokok
cinema bioskop
city kota
city centre pusat kota
class kelas
classical music musik klasik
clean bersih
clear (obvious) jelas
  (water) jernih
  is that clear? apa itu jelas?
clever pandai
clock jam

close *(near)* dekat
  (stuffy) pengap
  (verb) menutup
closed tutup
clothes pakaian
clove cengkeh
club kelab
clubs *(cards)* klaver
clutch kopling
coach bis
  (of train) gerbong
coach station setasiun bis
coat jas
coathanger gantungan jas
cockroach kecoa
coconut kelapa
coconut milk air kelapa
coffee kopi
coin uang logam
cold *(illness)* selesma
  (adj) dingin
  I have a cold saya selesma
  I am cold saya dingin
  it's cold dingin
collar kerah
collection *(stamps etc)* koleksi
  (postal) pengambilan
colour warna
colour film film warna
comb *(noun)* sisir
  (verb) menyisir
come datang
  I come from ... saya dari ...
  we came last week kami datang
  minggu lalu
  come here! ke sini!
compact disc kompak disk
compartment kompartemen
complicated sulit
computer komputer
concert konser
conditioner *(hair)* kondisioner
condom kondom

conductor *(bus)* kondektur
  (orchestra) dirigen
congratulations! selamat!
constipation sembelit
consulate konsulat
contact lenses kontak lens
contraceptive kontraseptif
cook *(noun)* koki
  (verb) memasak
cooker kompor
cooking utensils alat masak
cool sejuk
coral karang
coral reef batu karang
cork gabus
corkscrew kotrek
corner sudut
corridor gang
cosmetics kosmetik
cost: what does it cost? berapa
  harganya?
cotton katun
cotton wool kapas
cough *(noun, verb)* batuk
counter konter
country *(state)* negeri
  (not town) pedalaman
cousin sepupu
crab kepiting
cramp kram
crayfish udang karang
cream krim
credit card kartu kredit
crew awak kapal
crisps keripik
crocodile buaya
crossroads persimpangan jalan
crowded ramai
cruise pelayaran
crutches tongkat ketiak
cry *(weep)* menangis
  (shout) berteriak
cucumber ketimun
cufflinks manset

cup cangkir
cupboard lemari
curls keriting
curry kari
curtain gorden
Customs bea-cukai
cut *(noun)* luka
  (verb) memotong

dad bapak
damp lembab
dance *(noun)* tarian
  (verb) menari
dangerous berbahaya
dark gelap
daughter puteri
day hari
dead *(animal)* mati
  (person) meninggal
deaf tuli
dear *(person)* sayang
  (expensive) mahal
deckchair kursi dek
deer rusa
deep dalam
delayed terlambat
deliberately sengaja
dentist dokter gigi
dentures gigi palsu
deny menyangkal
deodorant deodoran
department store toko serba ada
departure keberangkatan
departure lounge ruang
  keberangkatan
deposit *(verb)* menyimpan
develop *(film)* mencuci
diamond *(jewel)* berlian
diamonds *(cards)* ret
diarrhoea diare
diary buku harian
dictionary kamus
die meninggal
diesel disel
110

different berbeda
  that's different! itu lain!
  I'd like a different one saya mau yang
  lain
difficult sukar
dining room ruang makan
directory *(telephone)* buku telepon
dirty kotor
disabled cacad
distributor *(car)* delko
dive lompat
diving board papan lompat
divorced cerai
do melakukan
  how do you do? apa kabar?
doctor dokter
document dokumen
dog anjing
doll boneka
dollar dolar
door pintu
double room kamar untuk dua orang
doughnut donat
down: down there di bawah sana
drawing pin paku payung
dress *(noun)* gaun
drink *(noun)* minuman
  (verb) minum
  would you like a drink? anda mau
  minum?
drinking water air minum
drive *(verb)* mengemudi
driver pengemudi
driving licence SIM
drunk mabuk
dry kering
dry-cleaner's binatu kimia
dummy *(for baby)* dot
during selama
dustbin tempat sampah
duster lap
Dutch *(adj)* … Belanda
Dutchman pria Belanda
Dutchwoman wanita Belanda

duty-free bebas bea
duvet duve

each (*every*) masing-masing
  twenty rupiah each dua puluh rupiah
  satu
ear(s) telinga
early cepat
earring(s) subang
east timur
easy mudah
eat makan
egg telur
either: either of them satu dari mereka
  either ... or ... atau ... atau ...
elastic elastik
elastic band karet gelang
elbow siku
electric listrik
electricity listrik
else: something else yang lain
  someone else orang lain
  somewhere else di tempat lain
embarrassing memalukan
embassy kedutaan besar
embroidery bordir
emerald jamrud
emergency darurat
emergency brake rem darurat
emergency exit pintu darurat
empty kosong
end akhir
engaged (*couple*) bertunangan
  (*occupied*) dipakai
engine (*motor*) mesin
England Inggris
English Inggris
  (*language*) bahasa Inggris
Englishman pria Inggris
Englishwoman wanita Inggris
enlargement pembesaran
enough cukup
entertainment hiburan
entrance pintu masuk

envelope sampul
escalator eskalator
especially teristimewa
evening malam
every tiap
everyone tiap orang
everything segalanya
everywhere di mana-mana
example contoh
  for example contohnya
excellent bagus sekali
excess baggage bagasi yang lebih
exchange (*verb*) ganti
exchange rate kurs
excursion wisata
excuse me! maaf!
exit pintu keluar
expensive mahal
extension lead kabel sambungan
eye drops obat tetes mata
eye(s) mata

face muka
faint (*unclear*) tidak jelas
  (*verb*) pingsan
  I feel faint saya merasa pusing
fair (*funfair*) pekan raya
  (*just*) adil
  it's not fair tidak adil
false teeth gigi palsu
family keluarga
fan (*ventilator*) kipas
  (*enthusiast*) penggemar
fan belt tali kipas
fantastic hebat sekali
far jauh
  how far is it to ...? berapa jauh
  ke ...?
fare ongkos
farm pertanian
farmer petani
fashion mode
fast cepat

111

fat *(person)* gemuk
  (on meat etc) lemak
father bapak
fax *(noun)* fax
  (verb: document) memfax
feel *(touch)* meraba
  I feel hot saya merasa panas
  I feel like … saya ingin …
  I don't feel well saya merasa sakit
feet kaki
felt-tip pen spidol
fence pagar
ferry feri
fever demam
fiancé tunangan
fiancée tunangan
field lapangan
fig ara
filling *(in tooth)* tambal
  (in sandwich, cake etc) isi
film film
filter filter
finger jari
fire api
  (blaze) kebakaran
fire extinguisher pemadam api
fireworks kembang api
first pertama
first aid PPPK
first floor *(ground, storey)* lantai satu
fish ikan
fishing mancing
  to go fishing pergi mancing
fishing rod joran
fishmonger's toko ikan
fizzy bersoda
flag bendera
flash *(camera)* kilat
flat *(level)* datar
  (apartment) flat
flavour aroma
flea kutu
flight penerbangan
flip-flop(s) sandal

flipper(s) sirip
floor lantai
flour tepung
flower bunga
flu flu
flute suling
fly *(insect)* lalat
  (verb) terbang
fog kabut
folk music musik rakyat
food kaki
food poisoning keracunan makanan
foot kaki
football *(game)* sepak bola
  (ball) bola sepak
for untuk
  for me untuk saya
  what for? untuk apa?
  for a week untuk satu minggu
foreigner orang asing
forest hutan
forget lupa
fork garpu
fortnight dua minggu
fortress benteng
fountain pen fulpen
fourth keempat
fracture retak
free *(not engaged)* tidak dipakai
  (no charge) gratis
freezer lemari es
fridge kulkas
friend teman
friendly ramah
fringe *(hair)* poni
front: in front of … di depan …
fruit buah-buahan
fruit juice sari buah
fry menggoreng
frying pan kuali
full penuh
  I'm full (up) saya kenyang
full board sewa kamar dengan makan
funnel *(for pouring)* corong

funny lucu
  (odd) aneh
furniture mebel

garage *(for parking)* garasi
  (for repairs) bengkel
  (for petrol) pompa bensin
garden kebun
garlic bawang putih
gas-permeable lenses lensa tembus gas
gate pintu gerbang
  (at airport) pintu
gay homoseksual
gear *(car)* persneling
gear lever tongkat persneling
gel *(hair)* jel
gents *(toilet)* w.c. pria
get *(fetch)* mendapatkan
  have you got ...? apa anda
  punya ...?
  to get the train naik kereta api
get back: we get back tomorrow kami
  kembali besok
  to get something back mendapatkan
  kembali
get in masuk
  (arrive) tiba
get off *(from bus etc)* turun
get on *(bus etc)* naik
get out keluar
get up *(rise)* bangkit
gift hadiah
gin jin
ginger *(spice)* jahe
girl gadis
girlfriend pacar
give memberi
glad gembira
glass gelas
glasses kacamata
gloss prints foto mengkilap
glove(s) sarung tangan
glue lem
go pergi

goggles kacamata selam
gold mas
good baik
  good! baik!
goodbye sampai jumpa lagi
  (said to person going on journey) selamat
  jalan
  (said by person going on journey)
  selamat tinggal
government pemerintah
granddaughter cucu perempuan
grandfather kakek
grandmother nenek
grandparents kakek-nenek
grandson cucu laki-laki
grape(s) anggur
grass rumput
Great Britain Inggris
green hijau
grey abu-abu
grocer's toko pangan
ground floor lantai dasar
groundsheet alas tidur di tanah
guarantee *(noun)* garansi
  (verb) menjamin
guard penjaga
guest tamu
guide pemandu
guidebook buku pedoman
guitar gitar
gun pistol
  (rifle) senapan

hair rambut
haircut potong rambut
hairdresser's salon rias rambut
hair dryer pengering rambut
hair spray semprot rambut
half setengah
  half an hour setengah jam
half board sewa kamar tanpa makan
ham ham
hammer palu
hand tangan

handbag tas
handbrake rem tangan
handkerchief sapu tangan
handle *(door)* pegangan
handsome ganteng
happy gembira
harbour pelabuhan
hard keras
  (difficult) sukar
hard lenses lensa keras
hardware shop toko besi
hat topi
have punya
  I don't have ... saya tidak
  punya ...
  can I have ...? boleh saya
  minta ...?
  have you got ...? apa anda
  punya ...?
  I have to go now saya harus
  pergi sekarang
he dia
head kepala
headache sakit kepala
headlight(s) lampu besar
hear mendengar
hearing aid alat pendengar
heart jantung
hearts *(cards)* jantung
heart attack serangan jantung
heavy berat
heel tumit
hello halo
help *(noun)* bantuan
  (verb) menolong
  help! tolong!
her dia
  it's for her untuk dia
  give it to her berikan kepadanya
  her ... ...-nya
  her book(s) bukunya
  it's hers punya dia
high tinggi
highway code peraturan lalu-lintas

hill bukit
him dia
  it's for him untuk dia
  give it to him berikan kepadanya
Hindu *(adj)* Hindu
hire: for hire untuk disewakan
his ... ...-nya
  his book(s) bukunya
  his shoe(s) sepatunya
  it's his punya dia
history sejarah
hitchhike numpang
hobby hobi
holiday liburan
Holland Negeri Belanda
home: at home di rumah
honest tulus
honey madu
honeymoon bulan madu
Hong Kong Hongkong
horn *(car)* klakson
  (animal) tanduk
horrible mengerikan
hospital rumah sakit
hot panas
  (spicy) pedas
hour jam
house rumah
how? bagaimana?
hungry: I'm hungry saya lapar
hurry: I'm in a hurry saya tergesa-gesa
husband suami

I saya
ice es
ice cream es krim
ice cube es batu
ice lolly es loli
if kalau
ignition kontak
ill sakit
immediately segera
impossible tidak mungkin

in di
  in English dalam bahasa Inggris
  in the hotel di hotel
  in Jakarta di Jakarta
India India
Indian *(man)* pria India
  (woman) wanita India
  (adj) ... India
Indian Ocean Samudera Hindia
indicator penunjuk arah
indigestion salah cerna
Indonesia Indonesia
Indonesian *(man)* pria Indonesia
  (woman) wanita Indonesia
  (adj) ... Indonesia
  (language) bahasa Indonesia
  the Indonesians orang Indonesia
infection infeksi
information penerangan
injection suntikan
injury cedera
ink tinta
inn hotel
inner tube ban dalam
insect serangga
insect repellent obat pengusir serangga
insomnia tidak bisa tidur
instant coffee kopi instan
insurance asuransi
interesting menarik
interpret menafsirkan
interpreter juru bahasa
invitation undangan
Ireland Irlandia
Irish Irlandia
Irishman pria Irlandia
Irishwoman wanita Irlandia
iron *(material)* besi
  (for clothes) setrika
  (verb) menyetrika
is *see p6*
island pulau
itch *(noun)* gatal
  it itches gatal

its ...-nya

jacket jaket
jacuzzi jakusi
jam selai
Java Jawa
Javanese *(noun)* orang Jawa
  (adj) ... Jawa
Java Sea Laut Jawa
jazz jazz
jealous cemburu
jeans jin
jellyfish ubur-ubur
jeweller's toko perhiasan
job pekerjaan
jog *(verb)* joging
  to go for a jog pergi joging
joke lelucon
journey perjalanan
jumper baju sweter
jungle hutan
just *(only)* hanya
  I've just one left saya punya hanya
  satu lagi
  it's just arrived baru tiba

Kampuchea Kamboja
kettle cerek
key kunci
kidney ginjal
kilo kilo
kilometre kilometer
kitchen dapur
kite layang-layang
knee dengkul
knife pisau
knit merajut
know: I don't know saya tidak tahu
Komodo dragon komodo

label etiket
lace kain renda
ladies *(toilet)* w.c. wanita
lady wanita

lake danau
lamb domba
   (*meat*) daging domba
lamp lampu
lampshade kap lampu
land (*noun*) tanah
   (*verb*) mendarat
language bahasa
large besar
last (*final*) terakhir
   last week minggu lalu
   last month bulan lalu
   at last! akhirnya!
late: it's getting late sudah malam
   the bus is late bis terlambat
later kemudian
laugh (*verb*) tertawa
laundry (*place*) penatu
   (*dirty clothes*) cucian
laxative obat cuci perut
lazy malas
leaf daun
leaflet selebaran
learn belajar
leather kulit
left (*not right*) kiri
   there's nothing left tidak ada tersisa
left luggage locker lemari tempat
  simpan barang
leg kaki
lemon limau
lemonade limun
length panjang
lens lensa
less kurang
lesson pelajaran
letter surat
letter box kotak surat
lettuce selada
library perpustakaan
licence lisensi
life hidup

lift (*in building*) lift
   could you give me a lift? boleh saya
  numpang?
light (*not heavy*) ringan
   (*not dark*) muda
light bulb bola lampu
light meter pengukur cahaya
lighter geretan
lighter fuel minyak geretan
like: I like you saya suka anda
   I like swimming saya suka berenang
   it's like … seperti …
   like this one seperti yang ini
lime (*fruit*) limau
lip salve salep bibir
lipstick lipstik
liqueur likir
list daftar
litre liter
litter sampah
little (*small*) sedikit
   it's a little big agak besar
   just a little sedikit saja
liver hati
lizard kadal
   (*in house*) cicak
lobster udang karang
lollipop gula-gula
long panjang
   how long does it take? berapa lama?
long-distance … … jarak jauh
   long-distance flight penerbangan
  jarak jauh
lorry truk
lot: a lot banyak
lotus flowers bunga teratai
loud keras
   (*colour*) menonjol
lounge ruang duduk
love (*noun*) cinta
   (*verb*) mencintai
lover pacar
   (*music etc*) pencinta
low rendah

luck untung
  good luck! selamat!
luggage bagasi
luggage rack tempat bagasi di atas
  mobil
lunch makan siang

mad gila
magazine majalah
mail *(noun)* surat
make membuat
make-up rias muka
Malay *(man)* pria Melayu
  (woman) wanita Melayu
  (adj) … Melayu
  (language) bahasa Melayu
  the Malays orang Melayu
Malaysia Malaysia
man pria
manager manajer
many: **not many** tidak banyak
map peta
  a map of Jakarta peta Jakarta
margarine margarin
market pasar
marmalade selai jeruk
married sudah menikah
mascara maskara
mast tiang
match *(light)* korek api
  (sport) pertandingan
material *(cloth)* bahan
matter: **it doesn't matter** tidak apa
mattress kasur
maybe barangkali
me saya
  it's for me untuk saya
  give it to me berikan kepada saya
meal makanan
mean: **what does this mean?** apa
  artinya?
meat daging
mechanic montir
medicine obat

meeting pertemuan
melon semangka
menu menu
message pesan
midday tengah hari
middle: **in the middle** di tengah-tengah
midnight tengah malam
milk susu
mine: **it's mine** punya saya
mineral water air mineral
minute menit
mirror cermin
Miss Nona
mistake salah
  to make a mistake membuat
  kesalahan
monastery biara
money uang
monkey kera
month bulan
monument *(modern)* monumen
  (ancient) candi
moon bulan
moped motor bebek
more lagi
morning pagi
  in the morning di pagi hari
mosquito nyamuk
mosquito net kelambu
mosque mesjid
mother ibu
motorbike sepeda motor
motorboat perahu motor
motorway jalan tol
mountain gunung
mouse tikus
mousse *(hair)* mus
moustache kumis
mouth mulut
move *(verb)* geser
  (house) pindah
  don't move! jangan bergerak
Mr Tuan
Mrs Nyonya

much: not much tidak banyak
  much better/slower jauh lebih
  baik/lambat
mug cangkir
mum bu
museum museum
mushroom jamur
music musik
musical instrument alat musik
musician musisi
Muslim (*adj*) Muslim
mussels kerang
must: I must saya harus
mustard mostar
my … … saya
  my bag tas saya
  my keys kunci saya

nail (*metal*) paku
  (*finger*) kuku
nail clippers gunting kuku
nailfile kikir kuku
nail polish cat kuku
name nama
  what's your name? siapa nama anda?
nappy popok
narrow sempit
near: near the door dekat pintu
  near London dekat London
necessary perlu
necklace kalung
need (*verb*) perlu
  I need … saya perlu …
  there's no need tidak perlu
needle jarum
negative (*photo*) negatif
neither: neither of them tidak satupun
  dari mereka
  neither … nor … bukan …
  bukan …
nephew kemenakan
never tidak pernah
new baru
news berita

newsagent's kios koran
newspaper suratkabar
New Zealand Selandia Baru
New Zealander (*man*) pria Selandia
  Baru
  (*woman*) wanita Selandia Baru
next (*in line*) yang terdekat
  next week minggu depan
  next month bulan depan
  what next? apa lagi?
nice (*attractive*) menarik
  (*pleasant*) baik
  (*to eat*) enak
niece kemenakan
night malam
nightclub kelab malam
nightdress pakaian malam
night porter jaga malam
no (*response*) tidak, bukan; *see USEFUL
  EVERYDAY PHRASES p7*
  I have no money saya tidak punya
  uang
noisy bising
north utara
Northern Ireland Irlandia Utara
nose hidung
not (*with adj/verb*) tidak
  (*with noun*) bukan; *see USEFUL
  EVERYDAY PHRASES p7*
notebook buku catatan
nothing: there's nothing left tidak ada
  yang tersisa
novel novel
now sekarang
nowhere di manapun juga tidak
number nomor
number plate pelat nomor
nurse perawat
nut (*fruit*) kacang
  (*for bolt*) mur
nutmeg pala

occasionally kadang-kadang
octopus ikan gurita

office kantor
often sering
oil minyak
ointment obat oles
OK baik
old tua
  how old are you? berapa umur anda?
olive jaitun
omelette telur dadar
on ... di atas ...
one satu
onion bawang
only hanya
open *(verb)* membuka
  (adj) buka
operation operasi
operator operator
opposite: **opposite the hospital**
  di depan rumah sakit
optician ahli kacamata
or atau
orange *(colour)* jingga
  (fruit) jeruk manis
orange juice sari jeruk
orchestra orkes
orchid anggrek
ordinary biasa
other: **the other ...** ... yang satu lagi
  the other one yang satu lagi
our ... *(excluding person(s) addressed)* ...
  kami
  (including person(s) addressed) ... kita
  it's ours punya kami/kita
out: **he's out** dia sedang keluar
outside di luar
over *(finished)* habis
  (across) di seberang ...
  (more than) lebih dari ...
  over there di sana
overtake melambung
oysters tiram

Pacific Ocean Samudera Pasifik
pack: **pack of cards** satu susun kartu

package paket
packet pak
  a packet of ... pak ...
padlock kunci gembok
page halaman
pagoda pagoda
  (Balinese) pura
pain sakit
paint *(noun)* cat
pair pasang
Pakistan Pakistan
Pakistani *(man)* pria Pakistan
  (woman) wanita Pakistan
  (adj) ... Pakistan
palace istana
pale pucat
palm tree pohon palem
pancake panekuk
paper kertas
paraffin minyak tanah
parcel paket
pardon? maaf?
parents orang tua
park *(noun)* taman
  (verb) parkir
parrot burung nuri
parting *(hair)* belahan
party *(celebration)* pesta
  (group) rombongan
  (political) partai
passenger penumpang
passport paspor
pasta mi
path jalan kecil
pavement kaki lima
pay membayar
peach persik
peanut(s) kacang
pear per
pearl mutiara
pea(s) polong
pedestrian pejalan kaki
peg *(clothes)* gantungan
pen pena

119

pencil pensil
pencil sharpener perancung pensil
penfriend sahabat pena
peninsula semenanjung
penknife pisau lipat
people orang-orang
pepper merica
  (red, green) lombok
peppermint(s) permen
per: per night per malam
perfect sempurna
perfume parfum
perhaps barangkali
perm permanen
petrol bensin
petrol station pompa bensin
Philippines Filipina
photograph *(noun)* foto
  (verb) memotret
photographer juru potret
phrase book buku ungkapan
piano piano
pickpocket tukang copet
picnic piknik
piece potong
pillow bantal
pilot pilot
pin peniti
pineapple nanas
pink merah muda
pipe pipa
piston piston
pizza pizza
place tempat
  at your place di tempat anda
plant tanaman
plaster *(for cut)* plester
plastic plastik
plastic bag kantung plastik
plate piring
platform peron
play *(theatre)* sandiwara
  (verb) bermain

please *(offering)* silakan
  (requesting) tolong
plug *(electrical)* steker
  (sink) sumbat
pocket saku
poison racun
police polisi
policeman polisi
police station kantor polisi
politics politik
poor miskin
  (bad quality) tidak baik
pop music musik pop
pork daging babi
port *(harbour)* pelabuhan
  (drink) anggur port
porter *(for luggage)* kuli angkut barang
  (hotel) tukang angkat kopor
possible mungkin
post *(noun)* surat
  (verb) memposkan
post box kotak surat
postcard kartu pos
postcode kode pos
poster poster
  (outside) plakat
postman tukang pos
post office kantor pos
potato kentang
poultry unggas
pound pon
powder bedak
pram kereta anak
prawn udang
prefer lebih suka
prescription resep
pretty *(beautiful)* cantik
  (quite) cukup
priest pendeta
private pribadi
problem masalah
  what's the problem? ada apa?
public umum
pull menarik

puncture bocor
purple ungu
purse dompet
push mendorong
pushchair kereta anak
put meletakkan
pyjamas piyama

quality mutu
quarter seperempat
quay dermaga
question pertanyaan
queue *(noun)* antrian
  (verb) antri
quick cepat
quiet tenang
quite cukup

radio radio
radish rades
railway jalan kereta api
rain hujan
raincoat jas hujan
raisins kismis
raspberry frambos
rare *(uncommon)* jarang
  (steak) setengah matang
rat tikus
razor blade silet
read membaca
reading lamp lampu baca
  (bedside) lampu tempat tidur
ready siap
rear light(s) lampu belakang
receipt kwitansi
receptionist penerima tamu
record *(music)* piringan hitam
  (sporting etc) rekor
record player gramofon
record shop toko piringan hitam
red merah
refreshments hidangan ringan
registered letter surat tercatat
relative *(noun)* kerabat

relax bersantai
religion agama
remember ingat
  I don't remember saya tidak ingat
rent *(verb)* menyewa
reservation pesanan tempat
rest *(noun: remainder)* sisa
  (verb: relax) beristirahat
restaurant restoran
restaurant car restorasi
return *(come back)* kembali
  (give back) kembalikan
return ticket karcis pulang pergi
rice beras
  (cooked) nasi
rich kaya
right *(correct)* benar
  (not left) kanan
ring *(wedding etc)* cincin
  (verb: phone) menelepon
ripe matang
river sungai
road jalan
rock *(stone)* batu
  (music) musik rok
roll *(bread)* roti
roof atap
room kamar
  (space) tempat
rope tali
rose mawar
round *(circular)* bundar
  it's my round giliran saya
rowing boat perahu dayung
rubber *(eraser)* karet penghapus
  (material) karet
rubbish sampah
ruby *(stone)* mirah delima
rucksack ransel
rug *(mat)* permadani
  (blanket) selimut
ruins puing
ruler *(for drawing)* penggaris
rum rum

run *(verb)* lari
runway landasan pacu

sad sedih
safe *(not dangerous)* aman
safety pin peniti
sailing boat kapal layar
salad selada
salami salami
sale *(at reduced prices)* obral
salmon salem
salt garam
same yang sama
  the **same dress** pakaian yang sama
  the **same people** orang yang sama
  same again, please yang sama
sand pasir
sandal(s) sandal
sand dunes bukit pasir
sandwich sandwich
sanitary towels pembalut wanita
sauce saus
saucepan panci
sauna sauna
sausage sosis
say berkata
  what did you say? apa kata anda?
  how do you say … in
  Indonesian? apa … dalam bahasa
  Indonesia?
scarf syal
  (head) tudung kepala
school sekolah
scissors gunting
Scotland Skotlandia
Scotsman pria Skotlandia
Scotswoman wanita Skotlandia
Scottish Skotlandia
screw sekrup
screwdriver obeng
sea laut
seafood makanan laut
seat tempat
seat belt sabuk pengaman

second *(of time)* detik
  (in series) kedua
see melihat
  I can't see saya tidak dapat melihat
  I see saya mengerti
sell menjual
sellotape® selotip®
separate *(adj)* terpisah
separated *(couple)* sudah berpisah
serious serius
serviette serbet
several beberapa
sew menjahit
shampoo sampo
shark ikan hiu
shave: to have a shave mencukur
  jenggot
shaving foam busa cukur
shawl syal
she dia
sheet seprai
shell kerang
shellfish kerang
sherry anggur seri
ship kapal
shirt kemeja
shoe lace(s) tali sepatu
shoe polish semir sepatu
shoe(s) sepatu
shop toko
shopping *(purchases)* belanjaan
  to go shopping pergi belanja
shopping centre pusat pertokoan
short pendek
shorts celana pendek
shoulder pundak
shower *(bath)* dus
  (rain) hujan
shrimp udang
shrine tempat suci
shutter *(camera)* layar
  (window) penutup jendela
side *(edge)* sisi
sights: the sights of … pemandangan …

silk sutera
silver perak
simple sederhana
sing menyanyi
Singapore Singapura
single (one) satu
  (unmarried: man) bujangan
  (woman) lajangan
single room kamar untuk satu orang
sister saudara perempuan
skid (verb) selip
skin kulit
skin cleanser pembersih kulit
skirt rok
sky langit
sleep (noun, verb) tidur
  to go to sleep tidur
sleeping bag karung untuk tidur
sleeping pill pil tidur
slipper(s) sandal
slow lambat
small kecil
smell (noun) bau
  (verb: something) mencium
  to have a smell berbau
smile senyum
smoke (noun) asap
  (verb) merokok
snack makanan kecil
snake ular
snorkel snorkel
so: so good begitu baik
  not so much tidak begitu banyak
soaking solution (for contact lenses)
  larutan perendam
soap sabun
socks kaus kaki
soda water air soda
soft lenses soft lens
somebody seseorang
somehow bagaimanapun
something sesuatu
sometimes kadang-kadang
somewhere di suatu tempat

son anak laki-laki
song lagu
sorry! maaf!
  I'm sorry maaf
  sorry? (pardon) maaf?
soup sop
south selatan
South China Sea Laut Cina Selatan
South-East Asia Asia Tenggara
souvenir suvenir
spade sekop
spades (cards) sekop
spanner kunci Inggris
spares suku cadang
spark(ing) plug busi
speak berbicara
  do you speak …? apa anda bicara
  bahasa …?
  I don't speak … saya tidak bicara
  bahasa …
speed kecepatan
speed limit batas kecepatan
speedometer spedometer
spices bumbu
spider laba-laba
spinach bayam
spoon sendok
sports centre pusat olahraga
sprain (noun) keseleo
spring (mechanical) pegas
  (season) musim semi
  hot spring sumber air panas
square (in town) alun-alun
  (adj: shape) empat persegi
stadium stadion
staircase tangga
stairs tangga
stamp perangko
stapler stepler
star bintang
start (verb) mulai
station setasiun
statue patung
steak bistik

123

steal mencuri
  it's been stolen dicuri
steamer (*boat*) kapal uap
steering wheel setir
steward pramugara
stewardess pramugari
sting (*noun*) sengatan
  (*verb*) menyengat
  it stings nyeri
stocking(s) stoking
stomach perut
stomach ache sakit perut
stop (*noun: bus*) perhentian
  (*verb*) berhenti
  stop! berhenti!
storm badai
strawberry arbei
stream (*small river*) sungai kecil
street jalan
string (*cord*) tali
  (*guitar etc*) snar
strong kuat
  (*taste, drink*) keras
student mahasiswa
stupid bodoh
suburbs pinggiran kota
sugar gula
suit (*noun*) setelan
  red suits you warna merah sesuai
  untuk anda
suitcase kopor
Sumatra Sumatera
sun matahari
sunbathe mandi matahari, berjemur
sunburn terbakar matahari
sunglasses kacamata hitam
sunny: it's sunny cerah
sunshade payung
suntan lotion minyak 'suntan'
supermarket supermarket
supper makan malam
supplement tambahan
sure pasti
  are you sure? apa anda pasti?
124

surname nama keluarga
swamp rawa
sweat (*noun*) keringat
  (*verb*) berkeringat
sweatshirt baju kaus
sweet (*not sour*) manis
  (*candy*) gula-gula
swim (*verb*) berenang
swimming costume pakaian renang
swimming pool kolam renang
swimming trunks celana renang
switch sakelar
synagogue gereja Yahudi

table meja
tablet tablet
take mengambil
take-away (*noun*) makanan bawa pergi
take off (*plane*) lepas landas
  (*clothes*) menanggalkan
talcum powder bedak talek
talk (*noun*) pembicaraan
  (*verb*) berbicara
tall tinggi
tampon(s) tampon
tangerine jeruk
tap keran
tapestry permadani dinding
tea teh
teacher guru
teak jati
tea plantation perkebunan teh
tea towel lap
telegram telegram
telephone (*noun*) telepon
  (*verb*) menelepon
telephone box kotak telepon
telephone call panggilan telepon
television televisi
temperature suhu
temple (*Javanese*) candi
  (*Balinese*) pura
tent tenda
tent peg pasak tenda

tent pole tiang tenda
Thailand Muang Thai
than dari pada
thank (verb) berterimakasih
  thank you/thanks terima kasih
that: that bus/man/woman
  bis/pria/wanita itu
  what's that? apa itu?
  I think that … saya pikir bahwa …
their … … mereka
their room kamar mereka
  their book(s) buku mereka
  it's theirs punya mereka
them mereka
  it's for them untuk mereka
  give it to them berikan kepada
  mereka
then (after that) kemudian
  (at that time) waktu itu
there di situ
  there is/are … ada …
  is/are there …? apa ada …?
thermos flask termos
these: these things barang-barang ini
  these are mine ini punya saya
they mereka
thick tebal
thin tipis
think pikir
  I think so say kira demikian
  I'll think about it saya akan pikirkan
  itu
third ketiga
thirsty: I'm thirsty saya haus
this: this bus/man/woman
  bis/pria/wanita ini
  what's this? apa ini?
  this is Mr … ini Tuan …
those: those things barang-barang itu
  those are his itu punya dia
throat kerongkongan
throat pastilles pastiles kerongkongan
through lewat
thunderstorm hujan angin

ticket karcis
tide pasang
  the tide's coming in pasang datang
tie (noun) dasi
  (verb) mengikat
tights stoking celana
time waktu
  what's the time? jam berapa?
timetable jadwal
tin kaleng
tin-opener pembuka kaleng
tip (money) tip
  (end) ujung
tired lelah
  I feel tired saya lelah
tissues kertas tisu
to: to England ke Inggris
  to the station ke stasiun
  to the doctor ke dokter
toast roti panggang
tobacco tembakau
today hari ini
together bersama
toilet w.c.
toilet paper kertas w.c.
tomato tomat
tomato juice sari tomat
tomorrow besok
tongue lidah
tonic tonik
tonight malam ini
too (also) juga
  (excessively) terlalu
tooth gigi
toothache sakit gigi
toothbrush sikat gigi
toothpaste pasta gigi
torch senter
tour tur
tourist turis
tourist office Kantor Pariwisata
towel anduk
tower menara
town kota

125

town hall balai kota
toy mainan
toy shop toko mainan
tracksuit pakaian lari
tractor traktor
tradition tradisi
traffic lalu-lintas
traffic jam kemacetan lalu-lintas
traffic lights lampu lalu-lintas
trailer gandengan
train kereta api
trainers sepatu olahraga
translate menerjemahkan
translator penterjemah
transmission *(car)* transmisi
travel agency biro perjalanan
traveller's cheque cek perjalanan
tray baki
tree pohon
trousers celana panjang
true benar
try *(verb)* mencoba
    (verb: taste) rasa
tunnel terowongan
turtle kura-kura
tweezers catut
typewriter mesin tik
tyre ban

umbrella payung
uncle paman
under di bawah
underpants celana dalam
underskirt rok dalam
understand mengerti
    I don't understand saya tidak
    mengerti
underwear pakaian dalam
university universitas
unmarried tidak menikah
until sampai
unusual tidak biasa
up *(upwards)* di atas
    up there di atas sana

urgent mendesak
us *(excluding person(s) addressed)* kami
    (including person(s) addressed) kita
    it's for us untuk kita/kami
    give it to us berikan kepada kami
use *(noun)* guna
    (verb) memakai
    it's no use tidak ada gunanya
useful berguna
usual biasa
usually biasanya

vacancy *(room)* kamar kosong
vacuum cleaner mesin penghisap debu
vacuum flask termos
valley lembah
valve katup
vanilla panili
vase jambangan bunga
veal daging anak sapi
vegetable sayuran
vegetarian *(noun)* vegetaris
vehicle kendaraan
very sangat
vest kaus oblong
video video
video recorder perekam video
Vietnam Vietnam
view pemandangan
viewfinder kaca pembidik
villa vila
village kampung
vinegar cuka
violin biola
visa visa
visit *(noun)* kunjungan
    (verb) mengunjungi
visitor pengunjung
    (tourist) wisatawan
vitamin tablet tablet vitamin
vodka vodka
voice suara
volcano gunung berapi

wait menunggu
  wait! tunggulah!
waiter pelayan
  waiter! *(younger)* dik!, bung!
  (older) mas!, pak!
waiting room ruang tunggu
waitress pelayan
  waitress! *(younger)* dik!, nona!
  (older) mbak!, bu!
Wales Wales
walk *(noun: stroll)* jalan
  (verb) berjalan
  to go for a walk pergi jalan-jalan
walkman® walkman®
wall dinding
wallet dompet
war perang
wardrobe lemari pakaian
warm hangat
was *see p6*
washing powder sabun cuci
washing-up liquid sabun cuci piring
wasp tawon
watch *(noun)* jam
  (verb) mengamati
water air
waterfall air terjun
wave *(noun)* gelombang
  (verb) melambaikan tangan
wavy *(hair)* keriting
we *(excluding person(s) addressed)* kami
  (including person(s) addressed) kita
weather cuaca
wedding pernikahan
week minggu
welcome *(verb)* selamat datang
  you're welcome sama-sama
wellingtons sepatu bot karet
Welsh Wales
Welshman pria Wales
Welshwoman wanita Wales
were *see p 6*
west barat
wet basah

what? apa?
wheel roda
wheelchair kursi roda
when? kapan?
where? di mana?
whether cuaca
which? mana?
whisky wiski
white putih
who? siapa?
why? mengapa?
wide luas
wife istri
wild pig babi hutan
wind angin
window jendela
windscreen kaca depan
wine anggur
wine list daftar anggur
wing sayap
with dengan
without tanpa
woman perempuan
wood *(material)* kayu
wool wol
word kata
work *(noun)* pekerjaan
  (verb) bekerja
worse lebih buruk
worst paling buruk
wrapping paper *(for parcels)* kertas
  pembungkus
  (for presents) kertas pembungkus kado
wrist pergelangan tangan
writing paper kertas tulis
wrong salah

year tahun
yellow kuning
yes ya
yesterday kemarin
yet: not yet belum
yoghurt yogurt
you … anda, *see p6*

your: your book buku anda
  your shoe(s) sepatu anda, *see*
   p6
yours: is this yours? apa ini punya
  anda?
youth hostel losmen pemuda

zip ritsleting
zoo taman satwa